SURVIVING MAHIGAN

J.O. SPENGLER

Paperback ISBN: 9798218124458

eBook ISBN: 9798218124472

ACKNOWLEDGEMENTS

This book is dedicated to my students, those who have inspired me, and taught me valuable lessons from the other side of the podium. The book is also dedicated to the memory of Herb Appenzeller and Kristi Schoepfer, exceptional people, valued colleagues, and Wake Forest devotees, who leave a legacy in the study of legal issues and safety in sport and entertainment.

I am extremely grateful to Brooklyn Jongeling, Allie Renee, Mary Allen Edgerton, and Caroline Spengler for their valuable feedback, and to Amanda (Let's Get Booked), for excellence in professional editing and cover design.

CHAPTER 1

"Be back to the room by five o'clock sharp," Logan heard his mother shout over the whine of the hotel hair dryer — one found bundled in a cord beneath the bathroom vanity. "We have a dinner reservation that we can't miss!"

He had begged, bargained, and pleaded with his mother for the past hour, desperate to have time away from under the watchful eye of his parents — and been granted two hours of independence for his efforts. This was only fair, he reasoned, as he was, after all, fourteen years old and able to fend for himself. He had taken a karate course and seen plenty of fight scenes in the movies, preparing him well, he believed, to fend off the perverts in the white vans, or wherever it was they were lurking these days.

Not wishing to risk a change of heart from his mother, he grabbed a key card and bolted from the room, the door sounding a "click" and soft "hiss," as it closed behind him. Free at last, he hurried down the hallway toward a bank of elevators. Ahead of him, he knew, was the most awesome resort waterpark he had ever seen. It had a dope waterslide, killer pool, a fun zone, and so much more. *This is one cool resort,* he thought to himself, *with a sweet name — The Mahigan Resort and Spa.* To Native Americans, he had learned, "Mahigan" means "wolf."

Logan marched forward, determined to make the most of his freedom in the short time he had. The only downside, one demanded by his overprotective mother, was that he had to stay in sight of his big sister, Jill, when he reached the pool.

I don't need a babysitter, he thought to himself. *If anything, I should be watching her.*

Logan reached the bank of elevators, stepped inside the one to the right, and punched the number that would let him off at the ground floor and a short walk to the pool.

Once off the elevator, he stood in awe of what lay ahead — the sight of the awesome pool, the smell of suntan lotion mingled with that of burgers cooking at a poolside bar, and one of his favorite tunes ringing out across the complex.

He reached the gate to the pool area and swiped his room key, hearing the satisfying sound of the lock disengaging. He quickly opened the gate, grabbed a plush white towel from the rack inside the fence, wiped his nose with it, and fast-walked to a row of lounge chairs with one occupied by none other than his annoying sister. She was easy to spot, with auburn hair and intense, green eyes, and a physique honed from hours in the gym, where she worked hard to stay in shape for the basketball team.

As he came near, he yelled out, "Hey Jill, you look really chubby in that bathing suit."

It gave him no small sense of satisfaction that his sister, who wanted to strangle him but didn't want to draw attention, could merely glare in his direction.

Logan threw his towel on the pool deck, ripped off his shirt and jumped in, directly in front of her, yelling the word that all those seeking peace and quiet at a public pool dreaded to hear — "Cannonball!"

Jill was caught completely off guard. Taking the brunt of the splash, she, along with her towel and t-shirt got thoroughly soaked. Shaking with rage, and momentarily losing her grip, she yelled, "Oh my God, Logan, you are such a brat!" as she grabbed her wet shirt and soft drink and stalked off.

Logan, for his part, laughed with glee as he wiped the water from his eyes and swam in circles, lost in the pure joy of the moment. *That was easy,* he thought with pleasure, *I got rid of the fun sponge. Now it's time to rock and roll.*

On his second turn, his eyes locked on the most incredible waterslide he had ever seen. He didn't know where his sister had gone. *Hopefully,* he thought, *she's gone back to the room and I'll be free of her for good.* These thoughts deeply satisfied him as he climbed out of the pool and made his way up the stairs to the top of the tower — and the entrance to the slide that would take him on the ride of his life.

This is awesome, he thought to himself, as he eyed the opening to the tubular slide ahead of him, guarded by some dork in a folding chair — the only thing standing between him and more fun than he could imagine. The guy looked like he hated his job and wanted to die — and probably wouldn't notice if a herd of elephants walked past. Logan immediately realized this presented a unique opportunity.

How cool would it be, he thought, *if I slid down backward. That stupid lifeguard isn't paying any attention.*

Seizing the moment, Logan ran forward, lowered his body into a crouch, and spun around through the opening to the slide. He could hear the guard yelling after him over the roar of the water as he disappeared into the darkness of the tube. "Too late, loser," Logan said to himself as he plummeted down the slide backward in a sitting position with his arms and hands extended in a vain attempt to keep his body stable.

The words had barely left his mouth when Logan's head struck the side of the tubular slide, sending shock waves of pain through his skull. Another turn of the slide resulted in a second impact, this time sending a sharp pain down the length of his neck. From there, fear and pain were the only sensations he would feel as he lost control of his body and whiplashed, like a rag doll, back and forth down the length of the slide. He was eventually jettisoned into the pool below where he came to rest, his last memory the relief of darkness enveloping him as he sunk below the surface.

***

Elaine Covington's stomach growled, reminding her of the dinner that she had been anticipating. *Where were those kids?* Her husband had just finished his shower and was no doubt drying off and putting the final touches on his preparation for their evening out. If the kids weren't back soon, they would be running late and she would have to call the restaurant to see if they could change their reservation. With anger replacing fear, she picked up her phone to call her daughter Jill.

"If they don't come soon, there will be consequences!", she vented aloud.

As she lifted her phone to dial, an incoming call lit up the screen. It was a number she didn't recognize. *Oh great,* she thought, *another solicitation call.* Her finger hovered over the red button to end the call, but she thought better of it. She sighed, and in a voice that would put the caller on notice that she wasn't interested in whatever it was they were selling, huffed, "Hello. What do *you* want!"

"Is this Mrs. Covington," came the officious voice on the other end, one that sounded oddly of compassion and concern, not at all like that of a telemarketer. For some reason, this sent a wave of fear and dread through her that was almost debilitating.

"Yes," she said without thinking, her mind already shifting gears to thoughts of her children.

"Ma'am, this is Officer Gibson from the Caldwell County police department. Are you the parent of Logan Covington?"

"Uh, yes," was her feeble response, as her mind raced. *Is he in trouble with the police? Is he hurt, or worse?* She waited for what seemed like a lifetime to hear more.

"We will need you and your husband to come to the hospital. Your son Logan has been involved in an accident and is currently in the ICU at Memorial Hospital."

Elaine, with tears welling in her eyes, dropped the phone to her side, and yelled, "Jerry, come quick. Logan is in the ICU. He was in an accident."

Jerry stepped into the room, and with an expression of unmasked fear, asked breathlessly, "Elaine, what is going on?"

"Hold on," said Elaine, let me put us on speaker. An Officer Gibson is on the line."

"What the hell happened?" yelled Jerry, into the empty space between him and the phone. "We are here at the resort." And then, without conviction, added, "We are safe here."

"Your son Logan was involved in an accident at the pool about an hour ago," replied the officer. "He incurred trauma to his head and neck and was involved in a near-drowning incident. A lifeguard performed CPR and revived your son, who was then stabilized and transported to Memorial Hospital. He is alive but in critical condition." Then he added, "We can meet you in the lobby in five minutes and transport you to the hospital if you would like."

"Thank you," said Elaine and Jerry in unison, the rising tide of anxiety threatening to overwhelm them. As they headed for the elevator, it occurred to Elaine that they still hadn't heard from Jill. She quickly dialed her number, but the call went immediately to voicemail. She tried five more times with no response. Her mind was whirring.

Could this really be happening? she thought. *The perfect vacation. An evening of family time over a great meal. All vanishing in the blink of an eye?*

"Jerry," she said, "All my calls to Jill are going to voicemail. Where could she be?"

Jerry, in a calm voice that betrayed an inner fear, said, "She is probably at the hospital with Logan — and they probably made her turn her phone off. Remember, she is the responsible one. I would bet the farm she is there safe and sound."

***

Elaine and Jerry arrived at the hospital with the police car's lights flashing and siren blaring. As the cruiser slowed, nearing the front entrance, Elaine had her hand on the door handle and was pulling it open. The car had barely made a complete stop when she leaped from the vehicle and ran toward the automatic doors leading into the hospital. Jerry followed close at her heels.

"My son, Logan!" Elaine screamed hysterically as she neared the information desk. "Where is he?"

While the staff stared blankly forward, unsure of how to respond, the officer quickly intervened. "Miss Covington, if you and your husband will follow me, we will go to the ICU to see your son." He had seen a lifetime of tragedy in his thirty years on the force and was well versed in handling distraught loved ones.

When they reached the ICU, they were directed by the floor nurse to Logan's room. They heard the thumping sound of the ventilator as they neared his room, and upon entering, saw that it was pumping precious air into Logan's damaged lungs.

Elaine, her head spinning, noticed to her dismay that Logan's head was bandaged from the emergency surgery needed to relieve pressure on his brain. Below his bandaged head was a brace that supported his injured neck. It was more than Elaine could take, and she wept uncontrollably as Jerry held her close, tears rolling down his own cheeks.

Silent prayers were given as they grieved for their son — and wondered anxiously why their daughter had not responded. It seemed that in a matter of hours, their perfect world had turned upside down and they were now in a world of the haunted, with sadness, fear, and grief their only companions.

CHAPTER 2

Nothing made sense.

Jill's head throbbed, and when she finally opened her eyes, darkness greeted her. Sharp, piercing pain stabbed at her wrists and ankles. It felt like something was cutting into her skin. *No, it is something more*, she thought. Whatever was causing the pain was also binding them closely together.

She screamed for all she was worth, but her efforts were fruitless, her screams muted by the thick, sticky duct tape covering her mouth.

Get a grip! thought Jill, as she willed her sharp mind to calm, and take stock of her situation. Raising her head, and peering through the semi-darkness, she realized that in addition to the duct tape over her mouth, she was bound at her wrists and ankles with zip ties — her hands and feet fully secured. Dressed only in a soaked t-shirt, with a bikini beneath, she shivered uncontrollably from both the cold, and a raw, relentless fear.

She kicked and rolled, inching closer to the feeble light coming from beneath the door. From this vantage point, she looked back, and could discern that she was imprisoned in a closet of some sort, likely a storage closet used by housekeeping. The pungent odor of cleaning agents served to reinforce this conclusion.

Jill fought through a brain fog to remember what had happened, recalling her little *brat* of a brother jumping into the pool and soaking her. She recalled her anger — and then how she had stalked off, wandering aimlessly for a bit, until she decided it was best to head back to the room.

Next came the memory of the elevator, how she had rushed to get on, focusing her attention on the nice man with the resort name tag. He was holding the door open for her with the palm of his hand. *What was the name on the tag?* The haze in her mind lifted, and she now saw the name clearly — "Johnny Grubbs." He was mostly bald, with dark brown eyes, and a salt and pepper goatee. Her near perfect memory had always been a point of pride for both her and her parents.

He had asked her something — oh yeah, which floor was I on — as the doors slid closed. I told him the floor number, fourteen, and turned away to avoid an awkward moment.

The memories came flooding back.

Wait, she thought, *something isn't right. I don't recall seeing any room numbers on the panel. Is my perfect memory playing tricks on me? Had I been in the wrong elevator?*

Her body jerked tight from the memory of what happened next — how strong hands, such very strong hands, had held her tight, with one placing a rag over her mouth. It smelled and tasted horrible. She had taken a deep breath to scream and…

Did I scream? I don't remember.

As hard as she tried, there were no more memories to recall. Just a blank space where memories should have been.

How long she had been unconscious was anyone's guess. It could have been hours. *My parents must be worried sick,* she thought, putting their wellbeing above her own.

Jill's thoughts then shifted to the pounding of music coming from somewhere nearby. *Someone must be having a party,* she thought, and hoped with all her heart that the party wasn't somehow connected to her fate. She silently wept as she considered the implications.

***

Justin had been severely reprimanded when his manager learned he was guarding the upper slide as the earlier tragic events had unfolded. *How did that kid slip past me? And why in the world did he slide down backward while sitting upright? It was crazy! And they blamed me!*

"Hey, it isn't your fault," he quietly told himself in between sips of beer at the pool-side bar. "At some point, kids or not, people have to take responsibility for their own actions." Regardless, the stupid manager *had* fired me, and said that because lawyers are sure to get involved, under no circumstances was I to talk to anyone about it. It was a classic case of covering your backside. He will probably lay *all* the blame on me, and I'll never get another lifeguarding job in this town.

Oh well, thought Justin, *it's back to flipping burgers until I find another way to earn beer money.* At least I still have a night of partying ahead.

He was sitting alone now, but just ten minutes earlier an older woman in a leopard-print cover up, smelling of expensive perfume, had slid her barstool close to his, and chatted him up. She had invaded his personal space, but he didn't mind. It was an age-old game that he enjoyed. She had bought him a beer and, after a few minutes of back and forth flirting and small talk, had made her move. It was an invitation to an exclusive party on the top floor in one of the luxury suites. He had heard about that floor, but never in his wildest dreams imagined he would be invited to go there.

"Heck yeah," he had said when given the invitation, his excitement overcoming his desire to act cool.

He remembered her saying, "The party starts at 9. I'd better see you there," as she pressed a key card in his palm, holding it there for a few beats as her fingers grazed his skin, quickening his pulse. She explained that he would need to use the card to access the private elevator leading to the top floor.

He knew he was no long-term catch for any woman, but he was young, tanned, and athletic, with dark brown hair and handsome features, so was at least good for the short term. Some of his friends said that he looked like Billy on *Stranger Things*, and even acted the same.

What did they call those older women who preyed on younger men? *Oh, yeah, "Cougar" is the word*, he thought, as a mischievous grin formed at the edges of his mouth.

With memories of the chance encounter fresh in his mind, Justin ordered a shot of whiskey, and another beer to provision himself for the night ahead. While he talked a big game, it belied the fact that he had moderate to severe social anxiety. Justin felt the burn of the whiskey as it washed down his throat, followed by the cold, bubbly sensation of the beer. It wasn't something that any doctor or therapist would prescribe, but it was his answer to stress. *That's better*, he thought dully, as the second gulp of beer flowed down his throat, washing away remnants of the whiskey's sting.

After some time alone with his thoughts at the tiki bar, he headed to the staff changing room, which was, as usual between shifts, mercifully abandoned. He didn't want to run into any of the other staff, or heaven forbid, a supervisor. After a long, relaxing shower, followed by his usual preparation for a night out, he donned some nice threads he had kept hanging in his locker in case he hooked up. He smiled, thinking of how his preparation had paid off.

Justin gathered his clothes and toiletries and threw them in a bag. He would not be coming back to work here, as his jerk of a manager had made clear to him. He certainly hoped "that Grubbs A-hole" wouldn't be at the party.

Justin thought about what might be in store for him as he entered the elevator. He now had the card from the mystery woman that would take him to the top floor. Stuffed in his pocket was also a key card that gave him access to other places at the resort, including most areas accessible only to staff. It was a stroke of luck that his manager had forgotten to ask him for it when he turned in his stuff. *Who knows when it might come in handy?*

Come to think of it, he thought, Grubbs did seem to be more than a little distracted earlier. *Not my issue tonight,* he thought, satisfied that he was free of him for good.

Stepping out onto the top floor, Justin immediately heard the pounding beat of 80s rock music. *Well, it was before my time, but certainly some of the best music ever produced*, he thought. He was sure that guests would complain, but this was where the big-moneyed guests stayed. *Money talks, right?*

The music seemed to be coming from the end of the curved hallway, so he headed in that direction — past the vending area with the sound of ice clinking in the machine. He walked slowly, building the courage to face the unknowns of the night ahead, down the curved hallway with expensive hardwood floors, leaving the vending area behind. Soon, he passed a supply closet on his right, one used for housekeeping. *What a thankless job*, he thought absently. *You couldn't pay me enough.*

A few steps past, he heard it — a faint noise coming from behind the door. *Could it be my imagination?* he thought to himself. Then he heard it again — "a rhythmic thud, thud, just loud enough to hear over the beat of the music down the hall.

Is someone in there? he thought. *Is a member of the housekeeping staff locked inside?* It doesn't make sense.

He turned toward the door to investigate, and swipe his key card, just as his former manager, Johnny Grubbs, and two of the toughest dudes he had ever seen, exited a room at the end of the hallway and headed his way. Justin turned to face them, palming his key card as he did so.

"What the hell are you doing here?" screamed Johnny, his high-pitched voice sounding like nails raking across a chalkboard. The sound made him cringe, but it was the guys who accompanied him that sent chills down his spine. They looked like mafia bodyguards and paid him the same kind of attention they might a bug they would brush from a pants leg and crush under foot.

"I'm, uh, here because I was invited," said Justin, his voice catching.

"Well, you have just been *uninvited*," Johnny said in his most menacing voice, one that left no room for argument.

"Uh, OK," Justin replied, turning on his heel and fast walking back down the hall.

Johnny and the two thugs laughed derisively at this cowardly act, and gave him no further thought.

As he rounded the curve in the hallway, Justin made a split-second decision and ducked into the vending room. As he stood there pondering what had just happened, he knew one thing for certain — something was terribly wrong. He just couldn't leave without knowing.

This is all just too fricking weird, he thought to himself.

Curiosity overtaking his better judgment, Justin silently stepped out of the vending room and slid along the wall to get a peek at what was happening back at the supply closet.

What he saw spiked his adrenaline and filled him with fear. The two goons, with their backs to him, were dragging a scantily clad young woman, bound and gagged, from the closet and were heading back toward the end of the hall where the party was raging. Grubbs was following closely behind, strutting down the hallway as if he owned the place.

Justin slipped back to the safety of the vending room, shaking uncontrollably. It didn't take a soothsayer to predict what would happen to this poor young woman. In fact, he now remembered seeing her at the pool lounging in the sun without a care in the world. This, for some reason, shook him to his core. He knew he had to contact hotel security. *No, screw security,* he thought decidedly, *I'm calling the police!*

CHAPTER 3

It had been almost a year since the incident, as I sat in my office at the university, and listened to the lawyer laying out a summary of facts surrounding the case. The boy had suffered serious and life-changing injuries that, although catastrophic, could have been worse. His lungs were functional, but he would never be able to run or physically exert himself due to damage from the near-drowning incident.

Not that it would matter really, given that he still couldn't walk without support because of the damage to his spine. He was recovering slowly, and the jury was still out on whether he would ever walk again unaided.

The facts, as recounted by the personal injury attorney, a Mr. Daniel Vining, were that the boy, Logan Covington, age 14, had slid backward, in a seated position, down a tubular slide at the resort where his family was staying, and struck his head violently against the side of the tube several times. When exiting the slide, he was likely unconscious and sank immediately to the bottom. Water quickly filled his lungs, as precious moments were lost due to the lifeguard's inattention. He had been underwater for more than a minute before he was noticed. He was then pulled from the water, where a lifeguard performed CPR until paramedics arrived.

I listened intently and scribbled notes on a piece of loose-leaf paper.

Tragedies such as this came with the territory when serving as an expert witness on personal injury cases. Despite having consulted on a multitude of cases, it never got easy.

The attorney continued, "So, would you be willing to provide us with your expertise, serving as an expert witness in this case? You come highly recommended, given your expertise in safety for this type of venue."

"Sure, Mr. Vining," I replied, sensing that I had an interesting case on my hands, and one where, at least on the surface, justice could be served by lending my opinion as an expert.

Also, I must admit, the case will result in some nice billable hours, I thought with satisfaction. I wasn't particularly greedy but who didn't need the money, especially when universities could be such penny pinchers.

Expert witnesses come in many shapes and sizes, with the main qualification being that a person has subject matter expertise. This could be obtained through experience — say, a doctor who has practiced in an area of specialty for many years — or through education and training, or some combination of both.

I coached sports and worked in entertainment venues earlier in life. Since entering the world of academia as a university professor a dozen years ago, I taught and studied safety issues as it pertained to sport, recreation, and hospitality. I had earned my stripes.

"Please call me Dan" he said pleasantly. "And send me your fee schedule and CV, so we can get you started. The case is Covington vs. Mahigan Resort Properties, et al."

"Sounds good, Dan," I replied, and then hung up.

My finger had hardly moved from pressing the 'end call' button on my phone when the sound of ringing startled me. It was an incoming call from the same area code and the first three numbers that had lit up my phone only a few minutes earlier.

Have they forgotten something? I thought to myself. *This is odd.*

Answering the call, I almost said, "Hello Mr. Vining," before a different voice came over the line. It was a woman's voice, only heightening my confusion.

"Hello," she said. "Is this Dr. Strickland?

"Yes," I replied.

"This is Janet Markridge," came the mystery voice. "I'm with the law firm of Taylor, Wray, and Miller, and represent a member of the Covington family in a personal injury matter. My colleague, Dan Vining, is representing another member of the family. He was going to reach out to you. Have you spoken with him yet?"

"Yes," I answered, with bewilderment. Two separate incidents involving the same family? This was a first.

"Our firm hopes to retain you as an expert on Dan's case, as well as another that I am pursuing on behalf of the family. The defendant in both cases is Mahigan Resort Properties. My colleague, Dan Vining, as you would know from speaking with him, is handling the negligence case involving the Covington's son, Logan. I'm handling a separate matter involving their daughter, Jill Covington, Logan's sister."

I waited, unsure of what to say as silence filled the air.

Janet broke the silence. "I understand this has probably caught you somewhat off guard, so let me explain. Both Logan, and his sister Jill, incurred injury on the very same day at the same resort. Strange, huh?

"Yeah," I quietly replied.

"Well, we thought so as well. Here is a synopsis of what happened. The Covington family was staying at the Mahigan Resort, one I'm sure you know about given its popularity. The

Covington's daughter, Jill, only 17 at the time of the incident, was abducted by a hotel employee who intended to traffic her. Luckily, a resort staff member witnessed the abduction and called the police. They arrived shortly after the call and found her in one of the top-floor luxury suite's bedrooms, thankfully unharmed. A hotel manager, Mr. Johnny Grubbs, and two low-level goons were in the room with her, waiting for a client, we think. They were immediately apprehended."

"Oh my gosh," was all I could say. A moment of gathering my composure helped me form more words. "Were criminal charges brought?" I asked.

"Yes. And a quick trial resulted in a criminal conviction for Mr. Grubbs. For his defense, it was argued that he suffered from a disability, one called Intermittent Explosive Disorder, also called IED, resulting in sudden episodes of impulsive, aggressive, and violent behavior that were beyond his control. He argued that his role in the abduction was solely done on impulse, one that was a function of IED. Long story short, the court didn't buy it, especially when it was brought out that he had an underage girl living with him — one that he had trafficked."

"He sounds like a monster," I said, catching my breath. "Thank goodness Jill was rescued in time. Did they catch the criminals behind it all?"

"Unfortunately, no. Mr. Grubbs and the two thugs refused to say who else was involved, so no-one else in their orbit has been apprehended or prosecuted."

Even though this was out of my subject matter expertise, I had to ask. "Couldn't the prosecutors use payment records to track the people who rented the suites?" There had to be some way to find out.

"After a lot of digging, they traced the payments to a third-party entity in Venezuela. The trail went cold there. The police raided the suites shortly after the incident. I'll get to the details of the abduction in a minute — but only lower-level criminals were apprehended. Everything was so well compartmentalized that it was impossible to learn who was ultimately responsible for the trafficking activity. It won't matter for your involvement, though, as we would like to hire you as an expert on the ensuing civil case against the manager and the resort properties."

My stomach churned as I imagined the trauma this poor young woman must have endured.

Thank God she was at least saved from something more horrific.

"So now," Janet continued, "with the criminal convictions behind them, the family has turned their sights on the wrongful actions of the resort and its employees. The criminal conviction will help our case on issues relevant to the manager's liability, since, as I'm sure you are aware, the burden of proof is higher in a criminal case than in a civil lawsuit."

I was aware of that fact, and had a decent understanding of the types of legal claims, and those that fell into the criminal or civil side of things. I had taught my students about the categories of liability, and how, in criminal cases, the standard of judgment dictates that the defendant must be found guilty beyond a reasonable doubt, meaning that it must be proved there is no reasonable doubt that the defendant committed a crime. The standard of judgment in a civil court, by contrast, is "preponderance of evidence," meaning that one side must present evidence that is more convincing than that presented by the other side.

I also knew that the question of double jeopardy — the Fifth Amendment prohibition to being tried twice for the same crime — does not apply if a civil suit follows a criminal conviction. Once a defendant has been found guilty under the criminal "reasonable doubt" standard, the "preponderance of evidence" standard found in civil courts is more easily established.

In most cases, judges determine that prima facie evidence — evidence that is sufficient, on its face, to find liability — is established by a criminal conviction. This means that a plaintiff has a good chance of succeeding on a claim for civil damages.

Pulling me from my thoughts, Janet continued.

"We know that the young woman, Jill, prior to being discovered in the hotel room, was chloroformed by the hotel manager in an elevator, and then bound and gagged, and locked in a storage room used by housekeeping."

"That is horrible!" I said with conviction. Then, donning my "hat" as an expert in hotel and resort safety, asked the first question that came to mind. "Didn't they have cameras in the elevators and hallways? This is standard practice for many upscale hotels and resorts."

"We have been to the hotel and spoken with the staff. Apparently, there were hallway cameras on all but the top floor. All the elevators, except for the one that serviced the top floor where Jill was taken — had cameras."

"My gosh," I said, incredulously, and then changed tack. "Didn't they perform background checks on hotel employees?"

"We'll be checking on that, as we continue to conduct discovery."

I knew that "discovery" in a legal case was the process of gathering and examining evidence — everything from physical evidence, to documents like policies and procedures, to depositions. I had been through my fair share of depositions — where you sit across from an attorney from the other side who bombards you with questions designed to extract your knowledge and expertise, and information that is valuable to their position on the case. My philosophy was to be honest, and found it to be true that "honesty is the best policy."

"We are bringing several legal claims on behalf of the family — a whole basket of them actually — to include the intentional torts of assault, battery, false imprisonment, and intentional infliction of emotional distress, as well as claims of negligence and gross negligence — carelessness and extreme carelessness — for the actions and inactions of the resort. Monetary damages will be pursued for both the pain and suffering endured by Jill, as well as that of her parents. We will also sue for compensatory damages, those expenses incurred for counseling and psychiatric services used by Jill and her family."

"That makes sense," I replied, imagining the horror that her parents must have endured.

Little did I know, the horrors were just beginning.

CHAPTER 4

I usually took learning about the initial facts of a case calmly, and my mind would shift immediately to the applicable policies, procedures, and industry standards — with a multitude of questions instantly forming in my mind.

Not this time, however. I sat there, with phone in hand, and pen poised above paper, struggling to maintain my composure while imagining the horror and sadness that this family had endured. As an aunt to two young children, it hit me especially hard.

After a moment of silence, Janet spoke again. "So, I realize this is a lot to put on your plate, with these two cases coming at you back-to-back. Feel free to decline if you feel it is too much."

"No," I said resolutely. "I would very much like to be retained on this case. This family needs justice to be served."

"My sentiments exactly," said Janet. "Our office will get you set up on both cases then. Did you agree to send Dan your fee schedule and CV for the negligence case involving Logan?"

"Yes, and I'll be sending those materials along with my retainer request right after this call."

"Great! We are thrilled to have you join our team as we work to seek justice for the family. Dan, as the lead on Logan's case, and myself as the lead on this case, will be working with you closely as we develop our separate legal strategies. Given the enormity of the issues, we anticipate one or both cases going to trial."

"I look forward to working with you both," I said. We then said our goodbyes, and the call ended.

My head was spinning with the images of pain and fear that both the children and parents had assuredly lived through. I knew that it could have been worse, and was thankful that it hadn't, but it was certainly terrible.

It was time, however, to get my head straight and prepare for my role as an expert — logically addressing the issues, policies, procedures, standards, and guidelines that would form the basis of my expert opinion. Much of it boiled down to the safety and security policies and procedures that were in place at the time of the incidents, and whether the resort staff followed them.

I also knew that I would need to do some sleuthing on my own to better understand the legal theories at play. I was thankful for the training I had in legal research from my law school electives during graduate school, and enjoyed hunting down legal cases that were like the ones I consulted on, to find case precedent. It was also rewarding to discover legal theories in journals and law reviews that came in handy when working on more complex cases for attorneys when they sought this type of assistance. Lexis and Westlaw were the internet search engines often used by those in the legal profession. Most universities subscribed to these services, and students and faculty could often use them for free.

Conveniently, my building was across the street from the law school, a sprawling complex with a first-class law library. There was a near-drowning case involving a child that I needed to consult.

I could have just sat at my desk and used Westlaw to find the case digitally, but I had the urge to move. It would allow me to think, and settle my nerves, given all that I was attempting to process. So, I got up from my desk, walked out of the building, and made my way on a beautiful, sun-drenched afternoon across the street to the library. Striding lithely across the law school courtyard, the sun reflecting off my shoulder-length ebony hair, and with my yellow-flecked, hazel eyes set on the path ahead, I felt fully alive.

Before leaving my office, I had scribbled a series of numbers and letters that most people would find indecipherable, on a slip of notebook paper. It read *Cater v. City of Cleveland*, 697 N.E.2d 610 (Ohio, 1998), and was the key to finding the case I needed.

Saying hello to Joe Hutcherson, the head librarian, and a good friend, I made my way upstairs to where the cases were held. I loved doing research the old school way, with the smell of old books, and the quietude that one can only find in a place of learning like a library.

Walking quietly through the shelves of books, I pulled out the slip of paper and consulted it. The first clue was one that would take me to my book of choice — the one that held the case I was seeking, *Cater v. City of Cleveland*. This case centered on supervisory issues in aquatics, and the provision of emergency care, issues that would be central to Logan's incident.

N.E.2d stood for "Northeastern Reporter, Second Series", which could be found by simply walking down the shelves of books until reaching the correct series of books. Finding the Northeastern Reporters, I then consulted the first number, #697, which stood for the volume. Looking down the row of books, it didn't take long to find the volume number, and I pulled the book from the shelf.

Taking the book to a table, I opened it to page number 610, the number after N.E.2d, and sure enough, the case name, *Cater v. City of Cleveland*, revealed itself. Legal research was very logical, and the geek in me really enjoyed it. I spent the next few hours studying this case and others, as I let my mind focus on issues, facts, and legal reasoning, pulling me from the nightmare faced by the Covington family.

As I sat in the quiet of the library, alone with my thoughts, I couldn't help but feel that a storm was brewing, one that would shake the very foundations of my life.

Sometimes I hate it when I'm right.

The day passed quietly, and soon turned to evening, finding me back at my condo, eating a meal I barely tasted, and pacing the floor, trying vainly to shake a feeling of impending doom. I'd always had a sixth sense for foreseeing trouble, but this time the feeling was exceptionally strong.

I had several hang-ups from unlisted numbers around dinnertime, which did nothing but strengthen my feeling of unease.

As the night wore on, I gave up on pacing, and prepared for bed. Sleep came hard, though, and I found myself tossing and turning, only able to drift off into the occasional fitful sleep.

Something in the far corner of my brain was sending off alarms. I couldn't quite grasp what was bothering me, but I just knew something troubling was sitting at the edge of my consciousness. Did it have something to do with these new cases?

My phone, which sat on the bedside table while recharging at night, sat silent. I picked it up and checked the time. It was 2 a.m.

In the next moment, something happened that would change the course of my life. My phone vibrated, the signal for an incoming call. I checked the caller ID and saw that it was from another unlisted number.

This had better not be a prank caller, I thought, as the tendons in my wrist bulged from gripping my phone so firmly in anger. I pondered whether to hang up.

No, it would be better to answer this time, and give a stern warning about calling back. I hit the green "answer" button, and soon wished I hadn't.

"Is this Dr. Strickland?" questioned the gruff voice on the other end before I had a chance to speak.

"Who is this?!" I said firmly, angered that someone would have the nerve to call me at such an hour.

Without responding to my question, the voice said, "It would be in your best interest if you didn't work for the plaintiff in the matters involving the Covington family — and then more firmly, and with menace — "Walk away and don't look back. You only get one chance."

"Now wait just a—" I started to say, my voice raised in anger and fear, but the caller had already hung up.

My heart was racing a mile a minute now, and I knew that any attempt at getting back to sleep would be futile. Pulling on a pair of jeans and a loose-fitting shirt, I headed to the den. I poured two fingers of Scotch from a bottle kept in the armoire and settled into a comfortable leather chair to think.

I only knew the basic facts about the case involving the young woman… Jill, but knew that it was serious. She had been abducted, and then rescued from some very bad people who supposedly meant to traffic her — an unidentified criminal enterprise.

My gut clenched.

They were warning me not to get involved. I wondered if they had scared off any other consultants or potential witnesses.

I would need to speak with the attorney leading the case, Janet, I recalled, once she was in her office. Part of me wanted to do what the voice had demanded — just walk away — while another part wanted to help the attorney find justice for the family.

My immediate responsibility was in the civil case though, which only involved the resort and the manager — not any hidden criminal enterprise. But what if they were afraid that we would dig up, or stumble upon, information that would uncover their operation? That had to be it. They wanted to intimidate everyone involved to keep the odds of being discovered to a minimum.

Another question came to mind. How did they know I was involved in the case? Was my phone call intercepted? If so, that would mean they had substantial resources. It may have been, however, as simple as finding out that I had been listed as an expert on the case, if the attorney had moved at lightning speed in listing me.

Regardless, I was on their radar, and that was a very bad place to be.

As I sat and thought about every aspect of the situation, a steely resolve formed within me. It was then that I made the decision. I would not let *anyone* intimidate me.

I would have to take precautions, but would provide my opinion and assistance on the case to the best of my ability. I owed it not only to Logan and Jill, and the Covington family, but also to anyone else who might be subject to the criminal actions of very bad people.

With what little remained of the night, I willed myself to sleep, only to be haunted by a vivid dream – one where I was captured at gunpoint, then bound and gagged, awaiting a fate that promised only misery and pain.

Morning, and the soft light that accompanied it, brought me awake and out of my torment. It was time to take control.

When 9 a.m. rolled around, the time I expected most attorneys would arrive at work, I called Janet, thinking my chances of reaching her were about 50-50. Maybe it was my day to play the lottery, because after dialing the number for the firm, I was put immediately through to her.

"Hello, Dr. Strickland," said Janet, a little too cheerfully, given my mood. "I'm glad you caught me. I have a deposition at ten and have some prep work to do. What can I do for you?"

"Thank you for taking the time to speak with me," I said a bit too tersely. Being threatened with your life, and a night of tortured sleep tended to do that to a person. I got straight to the point.

"Late last night, or more accurately, early this morning, I received a phone call from someone telling me to step away from consulting on the Covington cases — or else."

"Or else?" said Janet, the tone of her voice telling me the deposition was no longer her chief concern. She seemed laser focused.

"I believe the exact words were 'Walk away and don't look back. You only get one chance.'"

This statement was met with several long seconds of silence.

"Then, you should do just that. We don't want to put your life in jeopardy."

"Believe me, I don't want my life put in jeopardy either," I responded sincerely. "But…"

"But what?" asked Janet.

"But we need to seek justice for the Covingtons. I had a lot of time to think last night, and believe that whoever is ultimately behind the abduction doesn't want me, or anyone else, to dig up something that would tie their criminal enterprise to all of this. If I back out, they will just go after the person who takes my place, and they won't stop until you have no-one with the requisite expertise to support your case."

"I don't know," said Janet, her voice laced with indecision. And you won't like this, but I want to be fully transparent. Since you had agreed to be retained on the case involving the boy, Logan, we named you as an expert on *both* cases before you had agreed to the case involving his sister. We just felt that the probability was high that you would take both cases. Whoever these people are, they must have gotten wind of it. I am *so* sorry."

"You are right, but you still should have told me before listing me as an expert without my consent. At least this answers the question as to how they knew I was consulting on the case. I thought they might have had my phone or home under surveillance."

"We don't know how deep their resources go, so for now, I would like to take you off our list of experts. We can list you again, if you agree, once we get further along with discovery, and closer to a trial date. How does that sound?"

"Thanks," I said, exhaling a sigh of relief. "I definitely want to stay on the case though. I've made my decision."

"I certainly understand, and appreciate your willingness to serve, despite the threats. For the record, you still wish to work on Logan's case, right?"

"I do," was all I said.

"Good. I'm sure Dan will be sending you case materials to review shortly."

"Thanks Janet. I'll wait to hear from both of you. And good luck with your deposition."

"OK, thanks. We'll be in touch."

Janet hung up first, with me holding a silent phone and feeling only slightly better.

CHAPTER 5

The next six months passed quietly, with no more threatening calls or anything out of the ordinary.

The firm had been granted a continuance in Jill Covington's civil case, allowing them time to address outside influences. Dan, meanwhile, was pursuing the negligence claims that the Covingtons had brought on behalf of their son, Logan, with vigor. The case had the potential to result in a nice payday, and with a fifty percent contingency agreement, the firm stood to benefit from an even split of monetary damages awarded by a jury, or through a settlement offer.

For my part, being intimately involved in the case, and having poured over a mountain of paperwork, I was convinced that Logan's case had merit, and that my testimony would play a critical role.

Although Logan could now walk, it was only for short distances, and with the support of a walker, due to limited lung capacity and loss of function from partial paralysis. He might be able to live independently at some point, but would always need some manner of support. Apart from compensation for the "pain and suffering" that he endured, he would also receive support for his extensive medical bills, and the costs associated with his lifelong disability — compensatory damages — should he prevail in his lawsuit against the resort property.

Cases like these break my heart.

Early on, both sides had filed paperwork with the court — the complaint and subsequent responses, along with requests for interrogatories. Discovery produced a load of documentation — incident reports, records, internal memos, correspondence, depositions, photos, and more — all of which I read and analyzed.

The firm claimed in their initial filing that the resort and its employees were negligent in caring for the safety of their guests.

The resort was named in the lawsuit under a legal doctrine called respondent superior — basically meaning that everyone in the chain of command was responsible. This included the "higher ups" who were responsible for the actions of the front-line employees — the managers, supervisors and lifeguards who had made mistakes on that fateful day.

The resort upper management, for their part, also had direct responsibility in that they were responsible for developing and communicating safety policies and procedures for the resort. They also had the "deep pockets," unlike the low-paid staff, most of whom could be considered "judgment proof" and not worth suing given they didn't have much money.

Dan and his co-counsel, I had learned, had worked to reach a settlement up until the first day of trial, but failed to reach an agreement. It was a risk for the resort's attorneys to take the case before a jury, but the amount the plaintiffs were asking must have been too rich for their blood.

So, trial it is.

The attorneys had asked me to sit in the audience throughout the first week of trial to listen to the evidence and arguments — a strategy that would hopefully better prepare me for my testimony.

The first order of business, after the final legal maneuverings, was jury selection. Jury selection can be a long and tedious process, with most potential jurors hoping and praying they won't be selected, and can go back to their everyday routines of work and family. I must admit, however, that despite my own reluctance in the past, I knew it was my civic duty — and an important one.

The attorneys, in my opinion, did a great job with jury selection — a process known as "voir dire." The jurors who were selected provided good representation by age, gender, and racial and ethnic background.

The case was held in state trial court, given that both the Covingtons and the resort resided in the same state, and there was no federal question to resolve. I had testified in a few federal trials, one where a man from Iowa had traveled to Florida to visit a theme park where he was injured, and another where a person was injured at a national park. In the first case, the parties were from different states, — triggering diversity jurisdiction — while in the latter, a federal question was at issue. Both of those cases landed in federal court.

The courtroom had a comfortable feel. Unimposing in size, the room was immaculate, with natural light streaming in through high windows, and simple, wooden bench seating that had developed a rich patina.

You could say the trial officially started when Judge McDonnell, an attractive middle-aged woman donning a black robe, entered the room for the day that would feature opening arguments. Everyone immediately stood — except me. Lost in thought, I was a beat slow. But like a newcomer to a line dance, I quickly matched the movements of those around me, bolting from my seat, and blushing slightly from embarrassment.

Once we were seated, the judge made her greetings and went over a laundry list of housekeeping issues — things like timeliness, conduct, and the process the court would follow. This was mainly for the benefit of the jury, but good for all of us to hear. Her accent was crisp, with a hint of a midwestern upbringing, which matched her intelligent eyes and no-nonsense demeanor. She was clearly familiar with the case and understood its magnitude.

With the formalities concluded, and after a few hushed discussions among attorneys and trips to the bench to speak with the judge, the trial commenced in earnest. First up, following typical protocol in civil trials — was the plaintiff's attorney to give his opening statements.

Dan, who I had learned through working with him over the past months, was very good. He opened with a cordial and casual greeting, looking each jury member in the eye as he spoke. His easy going manner belied a sharp and cunning mind, and a pit-bull mentality. The man simply hated to lose.

"Good morning," he said, and then waited a beat.

Looking back at Logan, who was sitting near the table that he and his co-counsel were occupying, Dan said in a voice that conveyed deep sympathy, "My client, Logan Covington, needs your help. Logan was once a healthy, happy young man with a bright future ahead of him. As any child would be, he was thrilled to learn that his family would be going to a famous resort, the Mahigan, for a week-long vacation. Little did he, or his family know, the Mahigan Resort management would *fail* him and his family. A place that families visited, where they could let their hair down and feel safe, turned out to be anything but safe. In fact, the extreme carelessness of the resort management created a dangerous environment for their guests."

Dan continued by laying out the facts of the case, along with his legal argument, in a simple manner that engaged the jury.

With the full attention of the jury, Dan paused. He then delivered his final words.

"Mahigan," he said, looking directly at each member of the jury, "is a Native American word that means 'wolf'. Tragically, this Mahigan is a wolf in sheep's clothing — a seemingly safe place that hides an awful truth — one where the management of this resort has created a dangerous environment for families due to their careless and complete disregard for the safety of their guests. We intend to show the true nature of this 'wolf' over the next few days, and uncover the truth about how this tragedy could have easily been prevented."

When he concluded, I almost felt like clapping. He was *that* good.

The defense, for their part, were very good as well. The resort could clearly afford the best attorneys. This one was dressed impeccably in a three piece, gray, worsted wool suit, and sported horned-rim glasses that complimented his hawkish features and jet-black goatee. Their defense rested on the unfortunate "fact" that Logan, being old enough to know better, knowingly and with intent, slipped past the lifeguard on duty and slid down the slide backward before the lifeguard could react.

"What was the lifeguard to do?" asked the attorney rhetorically. "Jump in after him? That would have only made matters worse."

He has a point, I thought to myself. This is a weak point in the plaintiff's case, but at least they know that.

"Where were the parents?" the defendant's attorney asked in an accusing voice. "Someone should have been there to give him directions. He had earlier been disruptive in the pool, having intentionally soaked his sister and anyone nearby. And while I have sympathy for Logan, he was still a child, and in need of parental supervision, especially given his well-known propensity for horseplay and practical jokes."

I knew the legal defenses that the attorney was raising — comparative fault and assumption of risk. He was attempting to set the stage for testimony that would distribute the blame between Logan, his parents, and the resort. There was danger in placing the blame on a child — one who was permanently disabled — and losing the support of the jurors, so he had to tread lightly. It was also risky to place the blame on distraught parents who had been through hell. Still, the case could be made, and believed, that Logan and his parents shared some of the blame.

I also knew that the law in this state held that if a plaintiff was found to be more than 50% at fault in a case, they would receive nothing in monetary damages. If the defendant was more than 50% at fault, however, then they would divide up the percentage of fault between the parties, the plaintiff receiving the percentage of the total verdict that the defendant was deemed to be at fault.

I guess it made sense that if a person is injured and they sue, they shouldn't be awarded money from a lawsuit if they are mostly at fault themselves — but on the other hand, I was more in agreement with states that just proportion the fault between the parties and award the plaintiff some percentage of monetary damages, regardless of whether they are ten percent or ninety percent at fault themselves. Regardless of what I thought though, one thing was certain.

Dan had his work cut out for him to prove that the resort's negligence was the main cause of Logan's injuries. It was the classic blame game.

CHAPTER 6

My testimony had been scheduled for Friday and tomorrow was the day. Holed up at a hotel near the courthouse, I sipped a glass of wine and ate room service flatbread pizza while I thought back on the past few days.

Justin, the lifeguard, who attended the top of the slide, gave testimony earlier in the day. With his long black hair pulled up in a bun, and tanned, handsome features, he could have been a model for a fancy cosmetics company. Instead, he was, as he testified, currently working at a local fast-food restaurant. He lived in what he called a "basement apartment" with his mother, but claimed to be independent. He was not the best witness for the defense, but had been called by the plaintiff's attorney to testify, and was subsequently cross-examined by the defense.

Dan was relentless during his direct examination, finding every possible fault, and mercilessly extracting every detail about the incident that he could pull from him. I almost felt sorry for the guy.

In the end, Justin had said that he may have been daydreaming some, given how boring the job was, but that the kid, Logan, he now knew by name, had rushed past and turned backward before he could do anything to stop him.

The testimony, I recall, went something like this.

"Did you tell him to stop?" asked Dan.

"Yes," replied Justin.

"Was it before or after he reached the entrance to the slide?" queried Dan.

"Well, I guess he had already gotten past me when I told him to stop," said Justin.

"I see," said Dan in an accusatory tone. "Was he already sliding when you told him to stop?"

"Well," stammered Justin, "he was in the water."

"In the water?" Dan said in his most incredulous voice. And then, for good measure, repeated the question. "In the water?"

"Was he facing backward when he entered the water?"

"Yes," mumbled Justin, appearing as though he wanted to be anywhere in the world, even working at the crappy fast-food restaurant. Any place other than here.

"Was he standing or sitting?" asked Dan.

"Sitting," said Justin, caught in the moment and clearly just wanting this all to be over.

"I see," said Dan, setting the hook. "So, you had seen him enter the water near the entrance to the slide, turn while standing, and sit down facing backward. Only then did you tell him to stop — when he was already sitting and heading backward into the tubular slide. Is that correct?"

"Objection," the defense attorney yelled, spittle arcing through the air as it left his mouth. "Leading."

"Overruled," said Judge McDonnell calmly. "Let's hear what he has to say."

"Um, I don't remember everything that happened," Justin said in a vain attempt to avoid a response that would implicate himself.

"You said he was sitting backward when he entered the water at the entrance to the slide. I'm just asking how he got that way."

"Um, he walked up and sat down that way, I guess. But it all happened really fast."

"OK, so let's talk about something else for a minute."

Justin, looking quite relieved, simply nodded.

"Was this your first time guarding the water slide?" Dan asked, already knowing the answer. He just wanted the jury to hear it.

"Yes."

"In fact, it was your first day working at the resort in any capacity, correct?"

"That is correct, sir," replied Justin. "I hadn't worked there before doing anything else."

"Did you receive any training prior to starting the job?"

"Yes," said Justin, appearing more confident with this line of questioning. "I had training to become lifeguard certified through a course offered by the American Red Cross. I was also certified in AED and First Aid."

"Very good," said Dan, keeping Justin at ease. "Can you explain what AED means?"

"Um, I think it stands for 'Automated External Defibrillator.' You know, the thing that shocks the heart to get it to work again after it stops."

"Did you have any training on the specific … I mean any training that was specific to guarding the entrance to the slide?"

"Well, the day before I started working, um, actually working as a lifeguard, we had a half day of training that included staff introductions and getting familiar with the facility. Since I already had the lifeguard training, we didn't do any of that."

"I understand," said Dan patiently. "But what about any training that was specific to guarding the slide. Did you have any of that?"

"I didn't really expect to be guarding the slide. I thought I would be in one of the chairs. When I got there…"

"You mean the day you started, not the day of orientation, right?"

"Yeah, the day I started. When I got there, the pool supervisor, Ed Brady, told me I would be guarding the slide. He didn't really give me any training, just told me to sit up there and make sure that the kids didn't do anything foolish, that they slide the right way, and that I hold them back so that they don't slide too close together. You know, so they don't hit each other inside the slide, or when they come out the other end."

"Was that all the training you received?" asked Dan.

"Yes, that was about it."

"Did he tell you how long to wait between sliders, or to slide with arms crossed, feet out in front, facing forward, and on your back?

"He could have, but I really don't remember," Justin hedged.

"Last question," said Dan. "Did you feel well prepared after this 'training' to guard the slide?"

"Not really," said Justin, happy to deflect the blame on his good-for-nothing supervisor.

With Justin having said what he wanted the jury to hear, Dan ended his questioning, knowing full well that the defense would cross-examine Justin to "rehabilitate" his testimony. They didn't want to leave it with the jury that the resort staff were negligent in the manner and type of training they provided.

Finn Merriweather, co-counsel for the defense, made his appearance known, calling out, "Your honor, the defense would like to cross-examine this witness."

"Proceed, Mr. Merriweather," said Judge McDonnell in a deadpan voice.

Finn, with an air of confidence and conceit, sauntered up to the witness stand, and said in his most gentle voice, clearly an effort to calm this critical witness, "Justin, why don't you just take a deep breath and we can move on from the intimidation tactics exhibited by the plaintiff's attorney."

The opposite of his partner who had made the opening argument, Finn was middle-aged, donning a tan suit and colorful bowtie, and with a blue shirt that struggled to contain his amble belly — his buttons looking as though they would burst at any second. His glasses were the colorful type, with blue frames laced with neon orange.

"Hello Justin. I would like to personally commend you on agreeing to testify here today. And I apologize for the behavior of my colleague on the other side of the aisle."

Dan rose from his chair, then thought better of it, and sat back down. Finn had hit a nerve.

"OK," said Finn, "let's take a minute to talk about your training. *Would* you say that *no* amount of training would have prepared you for what happened that day? Or said another way, *no amount of training* could have prevented Logan from running past you, or any guard for that matter, and plunging backward down the slide, correct?"

"I, I guess so," said Justin, fidgeting in his seat and wringing his hands. He knew that the questioning was far from over.

Finn nodded, looked at the jury, and said matter-of-factly, "There was simply nothing you could have done."

Justin, shaking his head, replied, "Yes, that sounds about right," as he watched Finn turn, raise a hand, sigh, and say "No more questions" as he headed back to his seat at the table occupied by defense counsel.

"I would like to re-direct," said Dan, with a firmness to his voice that created a sense of foreboding.

As Dan approached the witness stand, he stopped and let the seconds tick by in silence. Justin fidgeted in his seat, rubbed his hands together, and rocked gently from side to side.

"Nothing you could have done?" asked Dan with a look of incredulity showing in his features.

Dan waited for a response.

"Well," said Justin, his voice shaking, "I guess that I could have walked away from the job after the pitiful training I received, but I needed the job, and the money."

"OK," said Dan, winding up for the fastball. "Was there *anything* you could have done to have prevented this horrible, life-changing injury from occurring?" Dan looked back to see the look of anger mingled with hopelessness on Logan's face, and then over to his mother, who sat quietly sobbing in the row behind Logan.

Dan raised his voice. "Could you have been at *least* paying attention? Could you have told Logan to stop at the line entering the water above the slide. Could you have then given him instructions on how to properly slide? Could you have—"

"Stop! Please stop!" Justin practically screamed. "I never should have taken the job. Ed Brady was a lazy jerk, and *his* manager was incompetent. I wasn't prepared, and I knew it."

Justin broke into a loud sob. "I just wasn't prepared."

"I have no more questions for this witness," said Dan, walking back to his seat, and leaving an inconsolable former lifeguard in his wake. I could tell that he felt sorry for the poor guy. But he had just helped his case tremendously, tying Justin's negligence to that of his employers. The case was moving in his client's favor.

Dan looked to Finn, who merely shook his head, seemingly resigned to accept his losses, and gear up for his examination of the expert witnesses.

Dan followed up with the direct examination of Justin's pool supervisor, Ed Brady, who testified that the training was thorough and adequate. To this point, he testified that Justin had been provided, on the day of orientation, a handbook that covered the rules of using the slide, and requirements for those guarding the slide. Ed Brady had further stated that Justin had been told to read and familiarize himself with the handbook before reporting to work the next day. He said, under oath, that he met with Justin and reviewed the procedures that Justin would need to follow.

Though dressed in a nice suit, and putting forth a good front, it was apparent that Ed was a heavy drinker — with a reddish, bulbous nose, slight tremor, and a mean temper lurking just beneath the surface.

Dan decided not to press him on the adequacy of training, as he would leave that to me as the safety expert.

Dan and his co-counsel had also brought in a psychiatrist to testify as to the mental and emotional damage incurred by

Logan and his family members, and a medical doctor to testify to the extent of Logan's physical injuries and dismal long-term health outlook. They painted a comprehensive and bleak picture of the impact the incident had on Logan and his family.

The last witness of the day was Logan's mother. Her role was to provide context and an emotional element that would hopefully resonate with the jury.

From her appearance, it was clear that she cared little about how the world viewed her. Her unpressed blouse, lack of make-up, slumped shoulders, and hair that hadn't seen a brush this morning, was testament to her distraught state of mind.

Dan, with sympathy evident in his voice and mannerism, said to Elaine, who had just been sworn in, her breath catching, and hand trembling as she recited the oath, "Thank you for your willingness to testify in front of the jury today. I know it must be very hard for you."

"It's OK," replied Elaine, her eyes darting between Dan and the jury. "I can do this."

"Would you tell the jury what your son Logan was like before the incident?"

"Well," said Elaine, tears welling up in her eyes. "He was just so happy and full of life. That is how I remember him.

He loved to climb trees, ride his bike, and play sports. He loved basketball most of all."

Elaine hesitated, her voice catching, and then said, "But of course he can't do any of that anymore. He mainly just sits in a chair, or in his bed and plays video games or does things with his phone."

"The incident has had a major impact on his life, then?"

"Yes," said Elaine, her eyes now focused on the jury. "Because of how careless the resort was in keeping my boy safe, he no longer smiles much, and I know he longs for how things were before the accident. It just… it just… breaks my heart. Our whole family feels it, and with all that is going on now with our daughter, it is just unbearable."

Dan paused as Elaine wept openly, tears staining her crumpled blouse.

Seeing the anguish on her face was almost too much to bear.

"One last question Elaine," said Dan, with a gentleness that seemed to lessen the flow of tears. "Has this created a financial burden on your family?"

"Oh yes," said Elaine, the question, and Dan's handling of the situation, helping to hold her emotions in check. "Both my husband and I have received counseling. And of course, our daughter Jill has as well. And then there are the medical bills. The costs are astronomical. We had to create a GoFundMe page to just pay the minimum of what we owe."

Elaine blew her nose, looked back at the jury, and said, "It has ruined our family — emotionally, physically, and financially. And you know what is worst of all — the resort has never reached out to us since the incident. They didn't even call to let us know he had been injured. We learned about it from the police. And to top it off, they never even said they were sorry."

"Thank you, Elaine," said Dan, looking back at the jury, where there wasn't a dry eye in the bunch.

With no more questions, the judge asked Finn if he would like to cross-examine the witness.

Looking as though he would rather pull a pregnant honey-badger out of her burrow, Finn simply shook his head and looked down at his papers. A long day of trial was over.

Reflecting on the busy day of testimony, I knew with certainty that I had to bring my A game. Dan, knowing what I would say from our many discussions about the case, was looking forward to my testimony. Finn, on the other hand, was likely looking forward to eviscerating me. My stomach churned as I thought about it. I studied my notes and paced the room — back and forth from the door to the window — while seeking to calm my nerves in the process. Later, sleep proved to be elusive, but the morning came quickly.

CHAPTER 7

I grabbed a coffee and a blueberry scone from the restaurant in the hotel lobby, then spent the better part of an hour reviewing my notes and consulting key documents from the case materials. When satisfied that I was as prepared as possible, I gathered up my belongings and walked to the courthouse, enjoying the crisp morning air and freedom of movement, knowing that I would be cooped up in the courtroom for at least the better part of the morning.

I arrived early and got a seat near the front, watching as the courtroom slowly filled and the trial resumed. I scanned the courtroom and saw all the familiar faces — those I knew to be Mahigan Resort's top brass, Logan's family and friends, the jury, judge and court officials, the attorneys, and staff, some of the experts from both sides, a few reporters, and a few lookie-loos.

There was also an obvious newcomer. He stood out not only because of his size, but also due to his brooding demeanor. He looked like a bouncer, or maybe a hit man, given his large, muscular frame, and ill-fitting, black suit. He sat halfway across the room, and when I looked his way, he turned toward me, his mouth parting in a rictus grin, bearing stained and crooked teeth. He was missing an incisor. I quickly looked away — a purely visceral response.

My heart leaped into my throat. This was no way to start what I was sure would be a very stressful day.

I was the last witness for the plaintiff's side, and since I was not listed for the defense, this would be my only appearance on the witness stand. The defense, I was one-hundred percent certain, would cross-examine me. That was the hard part, as I had rehearsed my responses to Dan's questions dozens of times and was ready for them.

Dan sought to use my testimony to bolster his argument that the resort had failed to meet the standard of care in providing for the safety of their patrons using the aquatics facility. He would ask me whether the negligence — carelessness — of the resort was the cause of Logan's life-changing injury.

When my time came to testify, I took my place on the witness stand and went through the swearing-in procedure. I took a deep breath, knowing that I would need to demonstrate confidence and keep my focus. If Finn smelled blood in the water — hesitance or forgetfulness — he would be all over me on cross-examination.

Dan approached me with an air of confidence. He smiled, glanced at the jury, and started with his first question — one that would establish my credibility. He asked me about my education and training, employment as a professor at a major research university, and my publications and teaching.

When I had finished talking about my background, and achievements in higher education, something that I was uncomfortable doing since I wasn't a boastful person, he followed up.

"That is an impressive list of accomplishments, Dr. Strickland." "Textbooks on sport, recreation, and hospitality safety, with chapters on aquatics, numerous scholarly articles on topics of safety and risk management in the field, and classes on the same. We appreciate your willingness to be here to share your expertise."

I simply nodded, glancing over to Finn who was furiously taking notes. It made my gut clench a little, knowing that he would be standing here soon, probing for cracks in the armor of my background and experience.

With my credibility established, Dan went straight to the heart of the matter. "Dr. Strickland," he said. "You have heard the testimony of the lifeguards, resort staff, and management, as well as that of the doctors, and engineer."

The engineer had taken the stand first this morning, right before I was called to testify. He testified as to the physical characteristics of the slide and the likelihood of head and neck impact when using the slide improperly. He was very good.

"Yes, I have," I said loudly and clearly, an important way to speak when providing testimony in a courtroom. There were plenty of ears that needed to hear what I had to say.

"And what did you learn?" asked Dan, couching his question in open-ended form. He knew that Finn would be belting out an objection if he asked a leading question to his own witness.

"Well, for one," I said with confidence, "I heard that Justin, the lifeguard guarding the entrance to the slide, felt that he had not been properly trained."

"OK," replied Dan, prompting my next response.

"Second, I heard he had not told Logan to stop at the entrance to the slide. And had not provided any warnings or instructions, other than telling him to stop once he was already past him and headed into the slide."

Dan interjected, just as we had planned. "Tell me, Dr. Strickland, what is customary, or what we might call 'industry practice,' when it comes to waterslide safety."

"Well, there is typically a shallow well or starting point well back from the entrance to the slide — the point where one would begin their descent through and down the slide. It usually has some sort of marking — perhaps a line which is not to be crossed until permission is given by the guard on duty.

"Did this slide have any such mark, or line, that one would not cross until given permission?"

"Yes, there was a line."

"So, at most facilities," Dan continued, "what happens? What does the guard do? What instructions are given? What is the procedure?"

"It is fairly simple," I said, and then regretted it. Finn would likely take advantage of this remark.

"The guard is responsible for stopping all guests before they begin their descent. They would be told to stay behind the line until told otherwise."

"Why?" asked Dan, his question laced with purpose.

"For several reasons. One, it holds the person there until the person sliding before them is safely clear of the slide exit. From my inspection of the slide, I found it had a green and red light at the slide entrance that was triggered by a motion-activated device at the slide exit. It lights up green when the prior person sliding has safely exited the slide."

"OK, what other reasons?" asked Dan.

"Second, the guard needs time to give instructions," I said confidently.

"And what are these instructions?"

"When sliding, lie flat on your back with your legs crossed and arms folded across your chest. You are to be seated forward behind the line, then when you are told to go, you push forward with your hands while in the seated position, then lean back flat, cross your legs, fold your arms, and slide."

"Were any of these procedures followed?" asked Dan in his most serious tone.

"No."

"And would Logan have been injured if the lifeguard had followed protocol and told Logan how to slide safely?"

"Probably not," I said. "The rules are in place—"

"Objection," yelled Finn, cutting me off in mid-sentence. "Calls for speculation and falls outside of the expertise of this witness."

Judge McDonnell hesitated for a moment before saying, "Sustained. The jury will disregard this testimony."

Unphased, Dan continued. "So, let's now shift our attention to the bottom of the slide where Logan exited. Did

you hear testimony indicating that Logan was unconscious —
or at least seriously dazed — when he exited the slide?"

"Yes," I replied.

"Do you have an opinion as to the actions of the lifeguard
who was responsible for the area where Logan exited the
slide?"

"Yes."

"Would you please share your expert opinion with the
jury."

"It is my understanding from prior deposition testimony
that Logan was underwater over a minute before he was
noticed and the lifeguard pulled him from the pool. It was
another ten minutes before paramedics arrived."

"And what is your opinion regarding the reasonableness
of the staff's response in Logan's situation?"

"Swimming pool operators should recognize and employ
the 10/20 rule."

"And what is this *standard?*" asked Dan.

"Objection!" shouted Finn. "May we approach the bench
your honor?"

"Sure," said the judge as Dan and Finn approached.

Finn whispered, "Your Honor, the 10/20 rule is not a
standard. It is a procedure, or perhaps a guideline that some
follow, but it doesn't create a standard of care in a legal
sense."

"Maybe not, said Dan, but it is called a standard by some aquatic groups, and a 'rule' by others."

The judge shifted in her seat, looking directly at Dan. "I don't want to confuse the jury on this point, as they have been instructed to consider the standard of care in determining negligence. I don't want it to be dispositive on this point."

"OK, your honor, I will call it a 'rule'."

Judge McDonnell turned to the jury and said, "Please disregard the term 'standard' as used by plaintiff's counsel."

Back in their places, Dan asked again, "Dr. Strickland, would you please explain the 10/20 rule."

"Yes. The rule represents the time a lifeguard has for scanning their assigned zone of the pool and to make a save if necessary. In this case, the lifeguard at the base of the slide was responsible for scanning the exit and the area proximate to it on both sides and straight beyond. The 10 represents 10 seconds —meaning they would perform a complete scan of their zone every ten seconds. The 20 represents 20 seconds — the amount of time it would take to respond and make a save."

"So, what would you deduce from what you know of the amount of time Logan was submerged?"

"Well," I responded. "I understand that Logan was at least underwater for a full minute, but probably more. It was the responsibility of the lifeguard to reach a victim and make a save within 20 seconds. Accounting for a few seconds of scan time, less for a slide as they should be watching to see when swimmers exit, they should have made the save in less than 30 seconds. They failed to make the save in over 60 seconds. That is an additional 30-40 seconds beyond the time they should have needed to rescue him."

Dan, thinking ahead, would use this in his closing argument — counting off 40 seconds to the jury, while telling them to think about being underwater and unconscious this amount of time — and the number of precious seconds wasted.

"Once he was out of the water and pulled onto the pool deck, do you recall what happened?"

"Yes, there was testimony from the lifeguard that she performed CPR, and at one point turned him to his side where he expelled water. She said she was relieved when he resumed breathing. I also understand that she provided assistance until the ambulance arrived six minutes later."

"A total of ten minutes from the time Logan went underwater, until the time that paramedics arrived," said Dan. "Is that a *reasonable* amount of time in your opinion, Doctor?"

"Well, sooner is always better," I said. "It is my understanding that management neither provided nor supported including EMT in their emergency action plan. Industry practice is to include local EMTs in emergency action planning. This would mean determining the approximate response time should they be needed, and periodic practice of the plan to ensure they are familiar with the location of the facility, and the most accessible and quickest entry point. Aquatics staff should be assigned who would meet EMT at the entry point to ensure they can get into the facility, and take them to the location of the incident. Time is always of the essence in situations like this, where there is a drowning or near-drowning event."

"Thank you, Dr. Strickland," said Dan kindly. "

Then, turning to the judge, he said, "Your honor, I have no more questions."

Finn was nearly on his feet before Dan had finished his sentence.

The wolf was on the hunt.

CHAPTER 8

I remained seated as Dan walked slowly back to his seat, only to be replaced with the loathsome Finn Merriweather.

"So, *Ms.* Strickland," said Finn by way of greeting, deliberately omitting my title of Doctor, a slight intended both to throw me off balance and lessen my credibility in the eyes of the jury.

I struggled with the decision to correct him, but remained silent. *No need to engage this hyena*, I thought.

"You said earlier, and under oath I might add, that the instructions and rules regarding the slide were 'simple'. You were also critical of my client for not providing enough training. Since it was, by your own admission, a *simple* matter to train someone to guard the slide, how are you finding the resort at fault? They required CPR and First Aid training along with training on the use of an AED, which Justin had acquired. They also provided Justin with a handbook that he was required to read prior to starting work — one that contained information relevant to guarding the slide. Is it your opinion that the information in the handbook was inadequate or factually incorrect?"

I could see where he was going with the questioning. While I found him to be quite distasteful, I had to admit that he was good at his job. I also had to admit the truth — the information in the handbook *did* cover all the necessary information and rules pertinent to safety.

"Well, no," I said, "the information in the handbook was not inadequate or incorrect, but Justin said that—"

Finn held up his hand to stop me from talking further and said, "Please just answer the question asked, Ms. Strickland."

Losing my cool, I said, more loudly than I intended, "It's *Dr.* Strickland."

"OK, whatever," Finn said dismissively, raising my blood pressure to an unhealthy level. He was getting under my skin.

"So, you are telling the jury that in your opinion, the handbook that Justin was required to read and use as guidance for the rules and instructions he was to give, was completely fine. The information it contained was adequate and correct for his assigned duties. I am saying this correctly, Ms. Strickland?"

"Yes," was all I could say as I found myself backed into a corner.

"I'm not sure it takes an expert, but I'd like to ask your opinion on another closely related issue. Justin was provided the handbook the day before he started work, and told that he was required to read it before his first shift began the next day. Is that how you understood it, Ms. Strickland?"

"Again, it's *Dr.* Strickland, and yes that sounds about right."

"Good. Your honor, the defense would like to submit the handbook as exhibit H into evidence."

"As you know, if you were paying attention, Ed Brady, Justin's pool supervisor, earlier testified that, in addition to the information provided in the handbook about guarding the slide, he also reviewed the procedure that Justin was required to follow prior to Justin starting work. Do you recall this testimony?"

"Yes."

"So," said Finn, as he wound up for the perfect curve ball, one he knew would surely cause me to whiff. "Justin had on-the-job training on the day of, as well as nearly 24 hours to read and study the handbook that contained everything he needed to know, to safely monitor the slide." Finn handed the book to me before he continued. "Would you please take a moment to look in the index and find where it talks about monitoring or guarding the slide. Then, when you have found it, please read the relevant section to the jury."

I wasn't certain where he was headed with this line of questioning, but did as Finn had requested.

"Ms. Strickland, having read it here and now, do you stand by your earlier sworn testimony that the information contained in the handbook that is of relevance to guarding the slide is adequate and correct?"

"Yes," was all I said.

"And do you know how long it just took you to find and read this information?"

"I wasn't timing myself, so no."

"Well, I was, and it took you four minutes and thirty-eight seconds. In your expert opinion, do you think it is *unreasonable* for the management of an aquatic facility to require their employees to read and study material that is critical to their job within a 24-hour period, when it would only take them less than five minutes to find and read that information?"

"The timing is not unreasonable, but—"

"I'm sorry Ms. Strickland, but I must stop you again. While we are on the issue of rules and instructions, while under oath and on the stand, please only answer the question asked. A simple yes or no answer will suffice. Is this something that you are *able* to understand?"

My blood was boiling again. Keep your cool, I told myself. Dan will have an opportunity to re-direct and then I can say more.

I couldn't help but roll my eyes, for the benefit of the jury, before saying, "Yes." *Boy, this guy is a real jerk.*

"So, I'll summarize for the jury. You have told us, under oath, that you agree that Justin was provided with a handbook that contained all the information he needed to guard the slide properly, and had plenty of time to read and understand the contents of the handbook as it applied to guarding the slide. You are also aware that he was provided with a review of procedures he was required to follow when guarding the slide. This was also told to him by his direct supervisor, Ed Brady, just before he headed up the stairs to the tower. Is this a correct summary, Ms. Strickland?"

"Yes."

"OK. Now, let's talk about your opinion where you are critical of the actions of the lifeguards who were guarding the pool and slide exit. Your opinion also addresses timing — the time it took to pull Logan from the pool, correct?"

"Yes."

"You were critical of the time it took the lifeguards to pull Logan from the pool, and cited the 10/20 rule. We will have an expert testify to this rule next week, but first want to be clear on your opinion. I'm going to summarize your opinion and then would like to ask some questions for clarification, OK?"

"OK."

"You broke the rule down into a ten second scan, and twenty seconds to make the save — that is, pull a victim from the pool and to safety. Then you testified the lifeguard was too slow in both noticing a problem and responding to it."

"Yes."

"OK, let's break this down further. First, the ten second scan. Finn, rotating his balding head on his chubby neck, imitated scanning the room. Can you explain this to me? If my head completes its scan, it should have completed the full ten second scan of the zone. Do I then start over or scan back from that point?"

"You would scan back from that point," I said, wondering where he was taking this line of questioning.

"And then, for the 20 second part, once a lifeguard spots a submerged swimmer, they need to get to them and pull them from the water within 20 seconds. Is that correct?

"Yes."

"Would you agree that it is difficult to see beneath the surface of turbulent water, such as that which flows from the exit of a slide?

"It could be, yes," I had to agree.

"Could the conditions at the exit of a slide make it more difficult to discover and save someone who was submerged beneath the water?"

"Perhaps, yes, but—"

"Please, just answer the question asked, Ms. Strickland. Then, while perhaps a good rule of thumb, wouldn't the 10/20 rule be more of a best case *guideline* under these conditions?"

Finn may not have realized it, but he had just waded into some dangerous territory for his client.

"The 10/20 rule," I said, seeing an opening to present my views, "was developed to provide a protocol for lifeguards to follow in creating a safe environment for swimmers. It can, however, be modified to take into consideration the conditions. For example—"

"Thank you, Ms. Strickland. The question, once again, only asked for a yes/no response," said Finn sternly.

"This one requires an explanation," I said resolutely.

Ignoring my answer, Finn turned to the bench and said, "Since I cannot get a straight answer, I have no more questions for this witness."

Dan rose and walked swiftly toward me.

"I would like to re-direct," he said.

"Dr. Strickland, and I will call you by your title, given that you have *earned* it — were you aware that Justin was not made aware of his lifeguarding assignment until moments before he started working at the waterslide?"

"Yes," I said, glad that Dan was providing important facts that Finn had intentionally omitted.

"Knowing this, do you think that the training the resort provided was adequate?

"No," I said, feeling renewed confidence. "Justin would not have known to focus on protocol in the handbook for monitoring the waterslide. And the training offered by Ed Brady should have been provided at the site — the top of the slide — where he could have gone over the protocols in the actual setting. He should also have then provided the opportunity for questions and stressed the most important safety considerations. The key would have been for this to have been done at the actual place — the top of the slide — where Justin would be working. This is how it is done at other waterparks and would be what I consider industry practice. Even simple instructions often need to be reinforced, especially where there are serious safety issues."

"Thank you for providing your expertise on this issue, Dr. Strickland. Now, as for the lifeguard at the slide exit, can you elaborate more on the 10/20 rule and how it would apply?"

"Yes, thank you. I've already stated that a good bit of time passed — at least an additional 30 seconds beyond the outside time allowed for a save according to the 10/20 rule

— before Logan was pulled from the water. And yes, conditions at the base of a slide *are* different from the rest of the pool, and would require something a bit different. That 'something' would be increased diligence in watching and listening for people exiting the slide. Given the turbulence and difficulty seeing beneath the surface, there would be an *increased* expectation of diligence among those guarding this area of the pool."

"And that brings up another good point, Dr. Strickland. Observation includes not only the visual but also the auditory, listening for the splash that comes from someone exiting the slide."

"Do you have anything else you wish to add, Dr. Strickland?"

"Nothing further," I said, knowing that sometimes it is best to leave well enough alone.

"Thank you, Dr. Strickland," said Dan.

I gave a brief smile and nodded my head, glad that I was able to not only get back on track, but to give Finn something to chew on.

Thankfully, Finn had no more questions.

The thug I had seen earlier, but had forgotten about in the heat of battle, was unfortunately still in his seat. We made eye contact and he once again gave me that sneering smile that exposed his missing incisor.

He silently clapped in a muted act of sarcasm.

CHAPTER 9

With plaintiff's examination of witnesses complete, Judge McDonnell called for a recess. By court procedure, the plaintiff was given the opportunity to go first when calling witnesses, upon the conclusion of opening statements. The defense would next be calling their witnesses, followed by closing statements from Dan, and then the defense counsel.

I was given the choice to stay and watch the remainder of the trial, but I had classes next week and needed to be there for my students. I think we also had a faculty meeting, one of those events that was dreaded by all.

In the hallway, I saw Logan, who gave me a one-armed hug from his wheelchair.

"Thank you, Dr. Strickland," he said with a crooked smile; his inner light momentarily piercing a veil of despair.

"Please, call me Renee. It is an honor to meet such a brave young man."

His mother, standing beside his wheelchair, stepped up and hugged me as though I was a life raft in heavy seas.

"Renee, we can't thank you enough for supporting us with your testimony. My husband and I want you to know how important it is to us."

I suppose that my importance to them was more symbolic than anything, given that my testimony, while likely helpful to the case, was less important than the fact that they perceived me to be on their side — which, in truth, I was.

"You are most welcome. I'm with you all the way," I said with all sincerity, offering a final hug to the distraught mother.

Overwhelmed with emotion, I turned to see Dan heading down the hall in my direction.

"Thank you for your testimony today, Dr. Strickland. You did great. I wanted to tell you that on the way out of the courtroom just now, Finn caught up with me, and outlined the details of a new settlement offer. Of course, he didn't admit defeat, saying instead that the resort felt sympathy for the Covington family and wanted to help them. It was a load of crap, but the offer is a good one."

I inwardly rejoiced for the family, as Dan gave me a warm smile and a firm handshake.

We parted company — leaving me with a strong sense of satisfaction, and perhaps something more.

I walked through the courthouse door, feeling the warmth of the sun on my face, and looking forward to a relaxed afternoon followed by a good — no, great — dinner and glass or two of fine wine. Nothing could dampen my spirits.

As I descended the courthouse steps, I realized I couldn't have been more wrong.

"Nice job, *doctor*," said the man with the missing front tooth and evil countenance who had approached me from behind. He had a slight lilting accent that could have been Australian, or Eastern European. I wasn't all that familiar with accents, so it was just a guess. Regardless, while the accent could have been considered pleasant if coming from another human, it only added to this man's threatening persona.

I turned to face him, determined not to be intimidated, and waited for him to continue.

He easily stood a good six feet, five inches, with a muscular build, and must have weighed well over two-hundred and fifty pounds. He towered over me, standing still and waiting for my reaction.

When he saw that I wasn't planning to respond, he grinned in a manner that held no humor. His next words sent ice through my veins.

"Well darling," he said, "your involvement with this family's legal matters seems to have come to an end. That is a good thing, don't you think, since this case seems to have taken a lot out of you. It would be *very unhealthy* for you to put yourself through more."

With those words, something broke within me — all those years of struggle to get where I had in higher education, compounded by the fact that I was a woman. All the times I had been overlooked or slighted, belittled and bullied, just as I had been earlier by Finn on cross-examination, came boiling up.

So, I turned to this mountain of a man, whose breath smelled like stale eggs, rotten fish, and tobacco, and said, "Screw you, Shrek! This is a free country and I'll make my own decisions. And I won't be intimidated by the likes of you!"

I was amped with adrenaline as I stood shaking in the shadow of this giant, whose demeanor had changed from cocky, to a tidal wave of meanness.

"You have chosen poorly, darling," he said evenly, while holding me in his gaze for several seconds. Then, before turning to walk away, he left me with ominous advice. "The world can be a very dangerous place. You should be *very* careful."

I stood there on the steps, frozen in place. Any thoughts of satisfaction with my participation in the trial washed away by the words of that thug, still ringing in my ears.

Yes, the world is indeed a dangerous place, I thought morosely.

I was awoken from my nightmarish reverie by Dan, who was bounding down the steps in my direction.

"Hey, Dr. Strickland, are you OK?

"Um, yes," I replied, but he wasn't convinced.

"I just caught the tail end of what looked like a conversation with a man who could only be described as *disreputable*. You seemed shaken up, so I came to see if I could help."

"Can we grab a coffee?" I asked, glad that I had not only an attorney to talk with, but one whose firm had a stake in whether I provided consultation on the Covington's next case involving their daughter.

"Sure," said Dan. "It looks like we have accepted the defense's offer for settlement. As I suggested before, it is a good one. I have as much time as you need now. There is a great coffee shop just a block from here if that works for you."

We walked the short distance in silence, as my nerves settled and I sorted through what I wanted to say. By the time we reached the coffee shop and had ordered, I was feeling much better. My former fear and indecision had been replaced once again by an anger fed by the intrusion on my sense of justice. No-one was going to bully me into running from that poor girl's case.

"Want to tell me what's going on?" asked Dan as we took our seats, and I enjoyed the first sip of a very tasty latte. Wiping the foam from my lips, I said, "I guess you could tell that the thug speaking with me on the steps was not a friend."

"Yep, it certainly looked that way," said Dan, genuinely concerned.

"Well, he strongly implied that I back off on helping your firm with the case involving Jill Covington, and followed up with a veiled threat. He told me that the world could be a very dangerous place and that I should be very careful."

"Whew," said Dan. "This is serious. You are the first witness that we have seen threatened, firsthand — and quite blatantly, I might add, being in broad daylight, on the courthouse steps. That is bold by any measure. I'm not totally in the loop on the sister's case, but have heard that some witnesses have withdrawn. I only know of two experts who remain on the case — an ex-combat veteran and older doctor who always seems unphased."

Dan waited a beat, and then added, "Our firm doesn't want to put you in harm's way."

"Hey," I said as a thought occurred to me. I know there are cameras both inside and outside the courthouse. "Do you think you could get an image of the man who spoke with me and provide it to the authorities to see if you can determine his identity?"

"I'll be straight with you on this. We have seen him before, lurking around one of our buildings, and had caught him on our camera feed. I saw him during the trial and knew he was the same person — probably there to intimidate us as well."

"I have to admit," I said. "it worked."

Dan continued. "We had his image run through the INTERPOL database several weeks ago and came up empty. He doesn't seem to exist on any other criminal databases either. Since he hasn't done anything yet that is technically illegal, we can't have him arrested. He walked a fine line with you just now, and is likely lying low."

Following my gut, I said, "I think that he would go to any length to keep me from working on Jill's case, and possibly testifying, given the chance — even a slim one — that my research might reveal the identity of whoever is ultimately behind Jill's abduction."

"We are just civil trial attorneys so unfortunately cannot offer you protection," said Dan. "I do know some people in law enforcement, though, if you want me to connect them with you. They may be able to help."

"Thanks for the offer, but I don't think they would expend protective resources on a veiled threat."

Then, with a mischievous grin, I added, "Calling him 'Shrek' did really seem to piss him off."

Dan gagged on his coffee as he laughed. "I guess it would." He placed the cup down. "Do you have a place to stay that no-one would suspect? It might be good for you to lie low for a while. And by no means will we put you in danger by listing you again as an expert on Jill's case. I'll talk to Janet about it. She works in another office complex, but we have an open line of communication on the Covington cases."

With direct eye contact, and a resolute look, I said, "Yes, I have a place to stay where no-one would find me. It is off the grid, and I'll spend some time there sorting things out. I have several other cases to work on, and classes to prepare for, so I'll stay busy. Also, I've made another decision. Please don't try to talk me out of it."

"What is that? asked Dan, already knowing — as any good lawyer does — the answer to the questions he asks.

"I still want to be retained on Jill's case. I want to help your firm bring justice to the family — and especially to that young woman. If she is brave enough to bring a claim, then I can certainly have the courage to lend my support."

Dan gazed intently at me for a full minute before speaking.

He finally said, "OK, I'll let Janet know. She will need to re-list you as an expert, for the purpose of discovery, so you need to be extra cautious now. Also, between us, I would increase your hourly rate. Call it hazard pay."

"OK," I said as the revelation of this commitment hit me, and I was filled with a strange high. It was the danger, I was sure, but I also knew that it would be short-lived, to be replaced with a steady diet of anxiety and fear.

I was thankful that I had a place to lay low that was off the grid. I needed to make a few calls, and get back to my condo and pack. I also needed to see if my graduate assistant could cover my classes for a few days, or for however long I needed to remain in hiding. There was a lot to accomplish in a short period of time.

Dan walked me to my car where we said our goodbyes, and I began preparations for any trouble that may lie ahead.

CHAPTER 10

I remained close with several camp friends from my college days. One of my best friends, Laura, had somehow managed to avoid social media and as far as I knew, didn't even text. We kept in touch, but only through the occasional phone call or shared meal when she was passing through.

One reason for her low profile was the celebrity status of her husband, a former NBA star who had launched a successful acting career after a torn MCL had sidelined him from basketball. They had houses all over the place, and one they rarely used, just an hour's drive from my condo in town. It was a small, but well-appointed cabin tucked back in the woods along the Green River in the southern Appalachian mountains.

I had visited only once, several years ago, when Laura had come alone. It was a rocky patch in their marriage — one they had since mended — and we had spent the afternoon drinking wine, laughing, and telling stories about simpler times. While I was there, she extended the invitation to visit, and told me where the key was hidden — beneath a piece of broken plank in a shed behind the house. She said that any time during the fall months, a time they always spent in LA, I could use it. The cabin was the perfect getaway, and should be beyond the reach of whatever criminal enterprise was threatening me.

I found my car in the courthouse parking lot, and drove back to my condo, checking the rearview mirror every so often to see if I'd been followed. It seemed that at least for now, no-one was interested in following me. Nearing my condominium building, I spotted the entrance to the garage, and wound my way to the lower level where my reserved parking space sat empty. For the first time since I had moved in, nearly two years ago, I didn't feel safe.

I drove to my parking spot and scanned the garage, then continued with a heightened sense of situational awareness as I exited the vehicle and made my way to the entrance to my condo — and safety.

Shutting the door and turning the deadbolt, I began my preparations. First, I created a checklist for what I would need to take with me and went upstairs to pack — striking through items as I crammed them in bags and suitcases. Adhering to the adage, 'Just because you are paranoid doesn't mean that somebody isn't after you', I took my laptop and flash drives, along with the hard drive to my desktop.

Before logging off, though, I emailed my teaching assistant, Andy, and told him I would need his help over the next few weeks with my classes — and that I would be sharing my lecture on negligence liability, the topic for the week.

I only taught one class this semester — a legal issues class for hospitality and event management students — given a course buyout I had received for a grant I had just finished up. Thank goodness it was a light semester. I considered telling Andy that I would be out of town, but decided against it. One never knew what might come back to bite you when you handed out too much information.

I then packed my most important documents; clothing, toiletries, and what few valuables and family heirlooms I owned. Next, I raided the pantry and bagged some essentials — Cheetos, chips, crackers and dip, peanut butter, bread, and some sweet treats — before moving to the fridge and grabbing a container of milk, a six-pack of beer, some sandwich meats, condiments, and cheese. I hope that my life in hiding will be short, but if I need food and can't leave the cabin, I want to be prepared. I didn't have a weapon, so if I am to survive and thrive, I will need to rely on my most powerful asset — my wits.

With my belongings piled by the door on a rolling cart, and ready to travel, I ran across the street to the local CVS and bought several burner phones and a few extra treats for the road.

I'm no super spy, but am a cautious person. If they could trace my calls and determine my location, I didn't want them to follow the movements of my personal phone. My cellphone will remain here. This has the added advantage of having them believe I am holed up in my condo — exactly what I want them to believe.

In the sub-basement to my apartment building sat an old Toyota Rav4 covered with a dusty tarp that my brother had bequeathed me when he took a high-powered job in the city. I pulled the cover off, momentarily choking on the accumulated dust, and set it aside. Piling the vehicle with my worldly possessions, I started the engine and was relieved to hear it come to life.

Donning a pair of dark sunglasses and my favorite faded red ball cap with the words *Coca Cola* emblazoned across the front, I pulled out of the garage and into the light of day. In case anyone was watching, I kept my face concealed by donning an N95 mask, as common as wearing a coat or hat today, even though the threat of COVID had waned. I saw no suspicious activity and breathed a sigh of relief when I was safely a few blocks away.

The trip to the cabin followed one-lane back roads with few cars, none of which had paid me the least bit of attention. I didn't need to be in the spy trade to know that I hadn't been followed.

Working from memory, I drove until I found the green faded mailbox at the entrance to the dirt road. There wasn't much out here — this far into the country — a place that, until somewhat recently, was inhabited mostly by moonshiners and folks that lived off the land. Gentrification had found its way even to the most remote areas, however, and riverside property, I knew, was at a premium. Here, private land was patch worked along the river, connected only by old logging roads and trails through the forest. Laura and Tony must have paid a small fortune for this piece of heaven.

Driving down the winding dirt road, kicking up a trail of dust behind me, I finally came upon the cabin. It was much as I remembered, a rustic cabin that disguised its true value — likely somewhere north of a million dollars — with its true beauty on the inside. The interior was paneled in black walnut, with large wooden columns spaced throughout. The fireplace was framed with river rock, while the stone floor was adorned with exquisite Native American rugs. Large leather armchairs and a comfy sofa complemented the living room. It was rustic elegance at its best.

I unloaded the car and unpacked my food and belongings, hurrying to my next stop — the well-stocked wine cellar.

It didn't take long to find an excellent bottle, a Château Margot of good vintage. Laura had told me to help myself to anything in the cabin — including, and especially, the wine — if I ever visited, so I took her up on the offer. I poured a glass of the delicious liquid, made a plate of cheese and crackers, and headed to the back porch overlooking the river.

The rhythmic, soothing sound of the water on the cool, sun dappled late afternoon, almost made me forget my predicament. I could now view my situation in a more objective manner, though there wasn't much to ponder. My commitment to the case was firm, and I wanted justice for the Covington family. The trauma they had endured at the hands of a well-known resort with incompetent and unethical management was difficult to comprehend.

I allowed my mind to rest and soak in the sights, sounds and smells of the forest. I suspected that peace of mind might be eluding me for the foreseeable future. Later, I drifted off to sleep and dreamed of being chased through the forest by a pack of wolves intent on devouring me. I was riding a dirt bike, and no matter how hard I tried, or how fast I drove, they remained at my heels. It was both maddening and frightening.

The next morning, I awoke to near silence — the only sound, the soft ripple of water from beyond the porch doors. Much to my surprise and delight, I found a fully stocked pantry and refrigerator/freezer with meats, eggs, vegetables, and drinks. Combining provisions left by my friend with my own, I prepared a decent breakfast. After feasting on scrambled eggs, fresh, hot Ethiopian coffee, and toast slathered with amazing strawberry preserves that I found in the cupboard, I fired up my computer to work on my lectures for the week.

My plan was to stay offline while at the cabin, and when my lectures were ready, drive to a point near the university and email the files to Andy, whom I would now notify of my absence. Once they had been delivered, I planned to take my computer offline and turn it off, then head back to the cabin.

Pretty smart, Dr. Strickland, I thought to myself.

CHAPTER 11

I felt right at home, sitting at Laura's rosewood writing desk. She was a budding novelist, and quite good at her craft. I peered at the screen, searching my files for the one that I wanted — it was the lecture on "negligence." Fortunately, I wouldn't have to re-invent the wheel with this one. I just needed to kick the dust off the earlier material, and add some improved fonts and case examples.

I typically started my lecture explaining negligence as a type of "tort," where a person is injured due to the carelessness of another — and how it consists of elements that can be listed simply as "duty," "breach," "causation," and "injury." A great resource for understanding tort law, and one I often consulted, was *Prosser and Keeton on Torts*, an authoritative text on the subject.

I began with the four elements of negligence, explaining each as I went along. As I prepared my slides, I wrote notes that Andy could follow. Sprucing up the first slide, I wrote that negligence lawsuits were also and, more informally, called personal injury lawsuits — where someone sued for money when they had been injured due to the carelessness of another.

The second slide dove into the elements of negligence, beginning with "duty." This first "element" of negligence was two-pronged, and each part needed to be proved by the plaintiff in a negligence case.

To find someone liable for negligence, I would tell my students, it must first be proved that a "duty" was owed to that person. I typed the example I often used in class about someone who was certified in CPR and First Aid. If a person held these certifications, I would ask rhetorically, would they have owed a *legal* duty to provide life-saving support for another person — let's say, at a hotel pool — when they, themselves, were guests at the hotel? The answer, I would tell my class, was "no." The person holding these certifications may have had an ethical or moral obligation to render aid, but not a legal one.

"What triggered the duty then?" I would ask next, followed by the answer, "A legal duty is triggered when there is a legal obligation, or responsibility, to another person." I would then change the facts of the hypothetical, and tell my students that if the same person had worked as a lifeguard for the hotel pool, then they would have had a legal duty to provide CPR when the situation called for it. In other words, they owed a duty of care to those for whom they were responsible — hotel guests using the pool.

Once it had been established that a legal duty existed, the second question I would raise centered on the standard of care, or what duty, or responsibility was owed? This was a critical issue in negligence cases, and one on which I was often hired to provide my opinion — just as I had recently, opining on responsibilities owed by the lifeguards and resort management.

The thought brought with it a jolt of anxiety that I worked to repress, returning my focus to the lecture.

Playground negligence cases, I believe, provide the perfect context for discussing the elements of negligence, and in particular, the standard of care. Where there is a playground at a city park, it could be argued that the city has a duty to provide a safe play environment for the public.

I recall a case where I was hired by the defense to render an opinion where a 5-year-old child was climbing on top of a jungle gym — or "domed climber" as it is often called. While climbing over the top, he slipped and fell through an opening in the support bars. The opening measured 7 inches by 8 inches, large enough for his body to pass through, but too small for his head to pass. As a result, he died by strangulation. I was asked to provide my opinion as to the standard of care for playground equipment.

I consulted the Consumer Product Safety Commission — CPSC, for short — a federal regulatory agency that protects consumers from dangerous products through safety publications, recalls and notices. The CPSC publishes a text that provides guidance on playground safety. It is called the *Handbook for Public Playground Safety*. The handbook provides recommendations on how to prevent head entrapment — the type of hazard that was at issue in the case I consulted on. The recommendation in the handbook is that openings in playground equipment be less than 3 inches, or greater than 9 inches in diameter — either too small for a child's body to pass through, or large enough for both the body and head of a small child to pass through.

This recommendation is based on scientific findings — in this case, average head, and torso measurements of small children of a certain age — determined by teams of scientists informing the work of another organization, the American Society for Testing and Materials, or ASTM for short. The result is a compilation of voluntary standards for playground safety — originating from the work and publications of the ASTM, and disseminated to the CPSC who boiled it down for use by the average person. Various professional associations backed up these recommendations and provided them to their user groups as well.

Thinking back, I recalled finding several cases with similar facts that I could use in my opinion. This is called case precedent, where earlier cases with similar facts are used in future cases to help the court make decisions. Each of these cases found liability for the park where openings in playground equipment were outside the specifications recommended by the CPSC and ASTM. From a reading of the prior cases, it appeared that case precedent had supported my opinion.

I also inspected other playgrounds in the community and found that none had outdated equipment of this type — with openings of this size. The reason for investigating whether the park had kept up with its neighbors, so to speak, on safety measures, was to see if they were meeting what is called "industry," or "community" standards, another factor that helps to determine the standard of care.

I had next examined the local health code, as well as the state code — also called a regulation, law, or legislation — and found that each required that the CPSC and ASTM recommendations be followed. At that point, I didn't need to look further.

The city had clearly breached its duty, or failed to meet the standard of care, in providing safe playground equipment — in this case, the jungle gym. By failing to meet code, the legal requirements in the state and local law, they were subject to *negligence per se*, the legal principle that held the defendant liable when they violate a statute designed to protect a person from the type of harm the law is designed to protect them from.

I was asked by the attorney working on the case to provide my opinion on the next element, following my analysis of the duty owed, and the breach of that duty. This element, called "causation," was straightforward. The improper dimensions of the opening, and failure to correct it, were the root cause of the death of the child. His body slid through the opening but his head did not, resulting in strangulation. In legal language, this was an example of "proximate cause" — where the injury was a direct result, or a reasonably probable consequence of the defendant's actions or failure to act.

And the injury? It was the unimaginable death of a child.

As my good friend and colleague liked to say, the defense was screwed with a capital "F." I wouldn't, of course, use this aphorism in class. It was cases like these that put me in the uncomfortable position of telling the attorney that their case was doomed, and that they should settle, if possible.

I typed notes for Andy to follow and added some fancy animations and touch-ups. Returning to my slide on the standard of care, I added "policy" as a determinant of standard of care. I recalled a case where a young man was injured in gym class during a supervised recreational basketball game. The student had gone up for a layup and was undercut by an opposing player. His head snapped against the floor when he fell, and he was momentarily dazed. The gym teacher pulled the young man from the game and helped him to the wall behind the court where he could sit and recover. While sitting by the wall, he became nauseous and dizzy, but remained conscious.

The school policy stated that if a sport participant sustained a suspected head injury, the teacher or supervisor was required to call 911 immediately. In this instance, the teacher waited until class was over — a good 30 minutes or so — and it became apparent that the student was seriously injured, before calling 911. At the hospital, it was determined that he had suffered a hematoma, bleeding on the brain. The delay in treatment — of which the time in calling 911 played a large part — resulted in irreparable brain damage to the young man. The school was found to be negligent, the bottom line being they failed to immediately call 911 when there was a suspected head injury — a requirement stated in their own school policy.

The policy was supported by the last piece of evidence that informed the standard of care in the case — recommendations from professional associations. Various medical groups recommended that 911 be called in the event of a suspected head injury, which in this case supported the policy of the school.

Satisfied that the lecture and notes were in order, I saved the file.

I would miss lecturing on this subject, but it would have to wait until the next semester. It was just too dangerous to go back to the university with someone gunning for me.

Just *how* dangerous I could not yet tell.

CHAPTER 12

At 9 o'clock sharp on Monday morning, I pulled out one of my burner phones and called the law firm, asking to speak with Janet. I knew something was up when the assistant who answered the call told me that she was in a meeting but had placed my call as a priority. She patched me through in less than a minute.

Janet answered breathlessly, "Dr. Strickland, I'm glad to know that you are OK, and hope you are in a safe place. I'm very glad you called."

This all seemed to come out in a single rush of words, sending up a red flag. I appreciated the compassion, but sensed there was something more.

"Um, I'm fine… and I'm in a safe place. Is there something I need to know?"

"OK, that is great news. Please keep your location private. It is best that even I don't know. You never know who might be listening to our conversation."

"That's good advice. I'll take it to heart," I said, though had already decided on this course of action.

"I have some unpleasant news for you," she said bluntly. "There was a massive fire at your condo last night at about 3 am. Your unit, as well as two others, were destroyed. The police have concluded that it was an act of arson."

I felt like the air had been sucked from my lungs as I sat and listened to this surreal story. All I could manage was a question: "Was anyone killed or injured?"

"So far, we know that an elderly man died in the fire, while a family next door to you had miraculously escaped unscathed."

I knew the family well — the Jamiesons — and thanked the heavens they were safe. Lynette and Steven had two young kids, and they were all super people. The older man, I didn't know.

This was all so senseless, and I burned with anger at the thought.

After giving me a moment to process the news, Janet picked up where she left off. "When we learned that it was your condo — we have staff whose job is to monitor police radio bands — we contacted the authorities and told them they could communicate with you through us. They will want to speak with you, but we bought you some time."

"Thanks. So, what happens next?" I muttered, as my mind continued to grasp the enormity of this revelation. I knew that something bad could happen, but had hoped that I was just being paranoid — using burner phones and going off-grid.

"Well, as we've said before, your safety is paramount. Dan spoke to me on Friday and I re-listed you as an expert witness in the case. He told me you are staying off the grid, and I honestly believed that whoever is behind this, wouldn't act so quickly and boldly. Once again, I underestimated the forces at work here. If you wish to walk away from this case, we certainly understand — and will make it very clear to anyone keeping track, that you are off the case."

"No," I said firmly. "As I said before, I am not backing down or away. The family needs my expertise. And if that poor girl is brave enough to face this, so can I!"

"OK then, here is the plan going forward," said Janet, getting straight to the point.

"We recently asked the judge to expedite the case and, over a weak objection from the defense, have been granted a trial that has been put on the docket for three weeks from today."

"Won't the defense have a good argument that they didn't have time to adequately prepare?" I asked.

"We don't think so," said Janet. "We filed a notice of claim some time before we first contacted you about the case, so despite the obvious *distractions* this case has posed, both sides have had plenty of time to conduct discovery and prepare for trial. The only missing pieces are your report, and another from our medical expert. The defense has made multiple settlement offers over the past few months, but the Covingtons prefer to take this to trial. I believe it is mainly about closure, and finding justice, for them."

Distractions? I thought. That was an interesting way to put it. It seemed callous, but I let it slide. Lawyers were very practical people.

"We have chosen and sequestered the necessary experts who have agreed to testify given the expedited nature of the trial. They will not be testifying to any matters that reveal the identity of the criminal enterprise behind all of this, so they should be safe once the trial is concluded. We don't anticipate your testimony to touch on any undiscovered parties behind the actions of the manager, either, so you should be fine in that regard as well once the trial has concluded. We believe they are only trying to bully and threaten our experts — and other witnesses — to keep the trial from happening at all."

Bully the witnesses? I thought to myself. *They burned down my frickin condo.* Janet was beginning to frustrate me.

"Other witnesses?" I asked, my thoughts returning to concern for others. "Have members of the family, resort employees such as Justin, and others been threatened?"

"You must agree to keep this confidential," said Janet, "but yes, they have. We are cooperating with the FBI, who are providing protection for the family, and have done our best to protect our other witnesses as well."

"So, the FBI is now involved. Why don't they go after the bad guys behind all of this?"

"That is a very good question," said Janet. "Again, this must be kept in confidence, but the FBI wants us to proceed with our civil case. They are waiting to see how things shake out, and whether the civil trial flushes out the criminal element behind it all. To be blunt though, this isn't our problem, as our goal in the civil trial is strictly to attain compensation for the pain and suffering endured by the young woman and her family."

"Is there more that you haven't told me?"

"Only that the FBI is also involved in the investigation into the fire at your condominium complex. Their involvement stems from the belief that whoever torched your apartment was associated with the criminal enterprise responsible for abducting Jill for purposes of human trafficking."

"I suppose that is a good thing," I said tersely, my mind traveling back to my own immediate problems.

Thank goodness for some forward thinking, I thought, as I remembered that I took everything that was important to me to the cabin.

"Getting back to the case," said Janet, pulling me back to my role, "we will proceed as would be typical for any case, but will need to take a clandestine approach to sharing information. First, when we are finished with this call, please discard your burner phone. It would be wise to use a different phone for each call and only call the number I will be providing in the case materials."

"Got it," I said, with more confidence than I felt.

"Also, your computer could be traceable, so to be on the safe side, all the case documents we will be sharing with you will be in print."

"That seems smart," I said.

"Don't say this out loud, but do you remember where you met with Dan?"

"Yes," I replied, remembering that I had only met with him once in person — after the trial — at a coffee shop down the street from the courthouse.

"Good, do you also remember the time of day when you met with him?"

"Yes," I replied again, seeing where she was going with this. *Dan must have told Janet about our meeting at the coffee shop*, I thought to myself.

"One of our legal assistants will meet you with the case materials tomorrow at a place two blocks west and one block north of where you and Dan met, and at the same time of day."

"Wow, I feel like a female James Bond," I said, lightly chuckling as the words left my mouth.

"I guess so, but remember that all of this is for your safety. Do you have any questions for me?"

"I appreciate the measures your firm is taking Janet, and for now, I'll reserve questions until I've had a chance to read through the case materials."

"Thank you," said Janet, tension evident in her voice. "And please call me immediately if you need anything else."

I promised and ended the call. Next, I pulled out the sim card, stepped outside onto the deck overlooking the river, and threw it into the rippling waters, where it was carried on its watery voyage downstream.

The next day, after downing a cup of strong black coffee and a few slices of toast, I took a deep breath, got up from my chair, and headed to the kitchen. Rinsing out my cup in the well-appointed kitchen, I went to the study and removed a key, and slip of paper from a secret compartment in the 18th century wooden desk — a hiding place that my friend Laura had told me about on my last visit.

It was time to leave, and I was timing my departure with Janet's instructions on when and where to pick up the case materials.

I walked back through the kitchen and out the side door, then headed for the barn a short distance behind the house, sitting at the edge of the forest. The decrepit old barn held a secret, and I knew that what looked like a run-down old building, was anything but that. I inserted the key into a rusted old lock securing the side door to the barn. It opened with surprising ease.

Removing the lock and setting it aside, I walked in to find an old cord hanging from a lone bulb in the ceiling of a dark entryway. I gave it a pull. The light from the bulb revealed a small room ahead, seemingly long unused and leading nowhere. It looked like a dead end, but I knew better.

Once in the room, a look at the wall to my right revealed what appeared to be an old rusted and locked utility panel. I inserted the same key used to open the outer lock and opened the panel. It, too, opened easily on well-lubricated hinges. I looked inside to find a high-tech keypad. The numbers, 1225, Laura's Christmas birthdate, were easy to recall, and I punched them in — to be immediately followed by the satisfying "click" of the lock disengaging.

Like something out of an Indiana Jones movie, the wall ahead, now revealing itself as a doorway, hissed open, promising that my journey would not end in this cramped, dusty room. As I walked across the threshold into another world, the building I entered illuminated with brilliant light, the hidden door silently closing behind me.

I gasped at the sight before me. The decrepit old barn, by outer appearances, was merely an illusion. The place was spotless, the floor gleaming as if it had been freshly scrubbed.

This was a showplace for some very special vehicles. Standing before me, as if they had just rolled off the assembly line, were a 427 Shelby Cobra, 1962 Ferrari 250 GTO, and McLaren F1. I removed my boots and, carrying them, walked quietly and reverently past these amazing works of automotive genius, while marveling at this special place — to an adjacent space that housed the vehicle I had come here to find. This area, the far wall of which comprised the bay door — rusted on the outside but all shiny metal on the inside, held the more "practical" vehicles — a Bentley SUV, Porsche Cayenne, and two bikes: a Harley Davidson Pan America, and Ducati Superlegerra V4.

The key was already in the ignition, so I pulled on my boots, slipped on Laura's helmet that hung from a handlebar, and jumped on the bike of my choice for today's task, the Harley Davidson. Laura and Tony had outfitted it with carrying containers in the rear. It was perfect for holding the case documents I would pick up. The bike would draw less attention than the Ducati, and was a fantastic bike that would serve my purposes to perfection.

I started the engine, donned my helmet, and pressed a button on the bike's dash that would open the bay door. Riding out of the mystery barn, the bay door slid closed behind me with hardly a sound. Making my way back to the side entrance, I turned off the light in the entranceway and locked the outermost side door.

Speeding down the gravel road leading to town, I took a deep breath and smiled.

Life had suddenly become quite an adventure.

CHAPTER 13

Piece of cake, I thought to myself, as the Harley ate up road beneath me. All I had to do was pick up the case materials and speed on back. *This whole "living on the run" thing is pretty cool,* I thought to myself. *Totally surreal — and dangerous… but totally cool.*

The Harley Pan Am was a great bike. I knew this because I was familiar with bikes. I had grown up on a farm in rural Kentucky and had taken to BMX racing at an early age. I was always competing with my three brothers, and as the youngest sibling — and a girl — had to work exponentially harder to gain respect. Now, as an adult, I rode on occasion for fun, but only when I could borrow a bike. I had settled into the humdrum life of academia and now rarely found the time — and couldn't justify buying something that I would seldom use. So now, flying down the road and experiencing the freedom that came from the feeling of my body piercing the open air, I was in hog heaven, no pun intended.

When I reached town, I decelerated and mentally mapped out my route through the narrow streets. Using the courthouse as my point of reference, I would go east past the coffee shop until eventually making the right-hand turn that would take me north a block.

Traffic was light and soon I was nearing my destination. When I reached the location where Janet's directions had led me, I saw there was a UPS store on the corner. *Great planning,* I thought. *This is a place that someone could hide with packages of documents in plain sight.*

I pulled my bike to the curb, parked, and waited. Even though it was probably overkill, I left my helmet on to conceal my identity and kept the bike running. I hadn't waited long when a short, mousy, overweight man in a blue, pin stripe suit came out of the store pulling a roller that carried several packages of documents.

The man in the suit greeted me and said, "Dr. Strickland, I have the documents pertinent to the Covington matter for you. May I help you load them?"

I noticed that beads of sweat had formed on his forehead, and he was surreptitiously inspecting his surroundings with noticeable anxiety. Before I could answer, he had removed a packet and handed it to me. Unlatching a compartment on the rear of my bike, I stuffed the first package in.

As I continued loading packages, I looked him over more closely and realized that he wasn't just nervous — he was terrified. I could only assume that he had not volunteered for this job. Just as I finished loading the final documents and locked the hatch, I spied a big pickup truck with a cattle guard on front—heading straight for us.

Most concerning of all, it was not slowing down.

The plan came together in a split second — for that was all I had. My mind computed that immobility meant death or serious bodily injury, neither of which seemed a good option. I knew that the man in the blue suit was no Olympic sprinter, and I was on a fast bike, so I would need to act as the bait.

With only a second or two to spare, and just enough time for the truck to change course, I tapped the throttle and crawled the bike onto the road.

I then chanced a look back, and to my great satisfaction, saw that the pickup had steered in my direction.

I may have just saved that dude's life, I thought. *He definitely owes me one.*

The downside to my plan, and hazard of starting off slow, was that the front end of the truck, and big metal cattle guard protruding from it, was now mere feet from the back of my bike. I could feel the morbid satisfaction of the driver as he envisioned delivering the killing blow. He had likely been told that I was a woman and thought that I didn't know how to handle a bike.

He couldn't have been more wrong.

I pulled hard on the throttle, and the Harley leaped forward, just as the truck was within a foot of ramming me, and ruining an otherwise great day. I sped down the street, knowing the Harley could easily outrun, and outmaneuver, the pickup. What I didn't anticipate, however, was the pickup blocking the intersection directly in front of me, and another approaching from a side street to the right. On the left was a row of shops fronted by closely spaced, large ornamental planters. *No place to go in that direction*, I thought.

I counted seconds in my head, and imagined angles, speed, and how much traction my wheels could hold.

The decision made, I let off the throttle and slowed the bike.

The truck with the cattle guard was, I could see with a quick glance in the mirror, running up fast behind me. It would, if given the opportunity, soon be running me down. The truck in my path was still blocking my way, and the large planters to the left provided no opportunity to pass. The truck to my right was still moving slowly toward the intersection, and would soon block any escape to the right.

It's now or never, I thought, with grim determination.

My BMX days, and the awesome handling qualities of this bike were the only things I had going for me. Well, that, and perhaps some lack of intellect — and overconfidence — on the part of my pursuers.

I gunned the engine, and the bike bolted forward, as if I was on some deranged kamikaze mission. In the next desperate act, I hit the brakes, silently counted to three, and pulled back into a wheelie an instant before colliding headfirst with the truck blocking my path.

The truck to my right stopped just before it closed off the only path left to me — and any hope of escape. The driver must have thought that I was a lunatic with a death wish, and like rubberneckers watching a wreck on the interstate, slowed to a stop in morbid fascination of what his eyes beheld. It worked to my advantage, creating an unlikely pathway for escape.

The crazy, and untested maneuver miraculously worked as my front wheel, hanging momentarily in the air as my forward momentum froze in time, tapped the front of the truck, then bounced off. It was a split second that would determine my fate, and I used it wisely, taking the opportunity to kick my left foot off the truck's bumper and, while balancing on the rear wheel, pull the bike sharply to the right. The rear wheel performed as intended, and rotated on the pavement, pointing me toward the narrow passage between the truck and planters on my right.

The Harley landed hard. Fighting to maintain my balance from the jarring impact of the front wheel hitting the pavement, I pulled the throttle fully and shot through the narrow gap and onto the street beyond, my heart racing.

I knew they couldn't get turned around in time to give chase, but didn't care. I don't remember all the details of the trip home — only that I was going fast — really, really fast.

Reaching the safety of the cabin, I unloaded the files and secured the bike under a covered shed behind the main barn. One never knew when a quick escape would be necessary. Scanning the area and neither seeing nor sensing anything out of place, I walked to the cabin, entered, and turned off the alarm.

I pulled a bottle of Pinot Noir from the cellar, walked back to the living room, and plopped down on the soft leather couch. I needed a minute to breathe.

A glass of wine later, my body felt more relaxed, but my mind remained restless. Like a kid with an unopened present, I just couldn't wait. I got up and grabbed a folder marked "Filings" from the table by the door. There was just one document that I wanted to see. It was the notice of claim. *There'll be time to review all the files tomorrow*, I thought, as I headed back to my place on the couch.

The notice of claim laid out the Covington's legal claims and included those Janet had mentioned earlier over the phone. The notice claimed the resort, manager, and others were negligent in failing to provide for a safe and secure hotel environment. In other words, it claimed that the resort was careless, and my job would be to provide my expert opinion on the standard resorts must follow for things like security cameras in hallways and elevators, security guards, and hiring practices for management.

The second claim was false imprisonment. Janet and her firm would have to prove there was an intent to confine Jill, and that it was wrongful. This one seemed open and shut to me, and my opinion on this issue was likely not needed.

The third claim was assault, which in civil cases means "threat" — the threat that a person would be touched in a harmful or offensive manner. Again, this one seemed obvious, as Jill would have been frightened beyond belief of the harm that would come to her at the hands of her captors. She also would certainly have believed in their ability to harm her. I knew that Janet would retain a psychologist who would opine as to the emotional trauma that Jill incurred.

A fourth claim, 'Battery', was another no-brainer, since it is a claim of harmful or offensive touching. Jill was clearly touched in a harmful or offensive manner, given that she was chloroformed, and then bound and gagged. Her physical damage, thank goodness, was nominal, but her emotional injury was significant.

Intentional, or negligent, infliction of emotional distress was the final claim. Here, Janet and her co-counsel would have to prove that the defendant's conduct was extreme and outrageous, and resulted in severe emotional distress, not only for Jill but also for her family. The manager's conduct certainly seemed outrageous to me. I had a few other words for it that included expletives, but pushed them to the back of my mind where such thoughts were best kept stored.

I sat back from the document and took a sip of wine, the fine vintage mingling complex flavors of cherry, raspberry, vanilla, and forest floor. The manager, Grubbs, was culpable on every count, I reasoned. The trick for the plaintiff would be to prove that the resort was at fault. I was sure there would be a lot of finger pointing and shifting of blame.

One thing was certain. The trial would prove to be very interesting.

CHAPTER 14

The next morning broke clear and cold. It was a perfect fall day, with temperatures, literally overnight, having become more Autumn-like. The weather was indeed crazy these days. After a quick breakfast, I sat down with a full cup of steaming black coffee and a large stack of papers to review.

The stack contained the notice of claim I had already pulled, multiple responses from both sides, and photos of the resort hallways, elevators, and of course, the area where the abduction occurred. Under the photos was a sealed envelope with what looked to be a USB flash drive tucked inside. The words 'video cam footage' on the envelope confirmed my suspicion. The stack also contained deposition testimony from the resort's upper management, mid-management, and hotel staff, along with testimony from experts for the defense.

I hadn't been deposed. Given the extenuating circumstances, the court, and surprisingly, the defense attorneys, had all agreed that a written report would suffice.

Depositions are an element of discovery that attorneys use to get information from a witness. They are sometimes very stressful and tiring. I recall, on past occasions, sitting across a conference table from attorneys, with a stenographer present, recording every word from the "question and answer" session. In one particularly difficult deposition, I provided deposition testimony for an entire eight hours. Most, fortunately, only lasted a few hours. Some attorneys could be quite aggressive, and even bullying, while others employed more subtle tactics. Either way, you had to bring your "A game."

My report was due by Friday at the close of business, 5 pm. This would give the defense two weeks to prepare, an amount of time the judge believed would be adequate to review it — or from the standpoint of the attorneys, pick my report apart and find ways to punch holes in my testimony at trial.

Taking a sip of the strong, Nicaraguan brew, I set the mug down and pulled the photographic evidence from the stack. The photos had been placed in small envelopes, with scribbled notes on the outside identifying the content within. Sorting through them, I could see that the person hired to take the photographs had left no stone unturned.

The first photo showed a view of the front, sides, and rear of the property, and included a Google map with an overhead view. These photos provided a nice perspective on the resort property.

The next set of photos were of the pool area, reception and front desk, and common areas. I studied these with a practiced eye and set them aside. I was thinking ahead, and eager to see the photos that would tell me where any hotel cameras were located.

Despite my eagerness to see the next set of photos, I decided to freshen my coffee with more from the pot. As I was topping off my mug, a sudden and unexpected cold shiver ran down my spine. What had triggered it, I didn't know.

Is it something I've seen in the photos? I asked myself.

Perhaps it was just the memory of the place, triggering thoughts of the horrors that the young girl must have endured there. Still, I'd take a closer look at the pool photos when I was finished examining them all.

The next set of photos was thick, and I quickly thumbed through the stack, seeing the same key feature in all of them. The stack contained photos of a hallway from each floor. To my satisfaction, each had security cameras placed at strategic intervals to ensure complete coverage of their respective hallways — their black domes indicating a 360-degree view. The only missing hallway photo was that of the top floor, which, of course, was of most interest since it is where the abduction occurred. It was in another envelope further in the stack, along with other photos of the floor where Jill had been so cruelly held against her will.

Pulling out my writing pad, I made notes as questions cascaded through my now highly wired brain.

Were the cameras video only? I knew that privacy laws prohibited cameras in private areas, such as hotel rooms and locker rooms, and those in public areas often could not include sound.

Were the cameras turned on at the time of the incident, and what were the resort's policies and procedures for accessing and viewing videos of public areas?

Was a hotel employee watching any of the videos at the time of the incident?

I couldn't wait to see the video footage as my mind processed all that I was seeing.

The next set of photos showed the inside of eleven different elevators — the total number of elevators that serviced the various wings of the high-rise resort building. All but one of the photos, the one marked "location of first incident — chloroform" had security cameras. The cameras were small and unobtrusive, but easy to find if you knew where to look.

I finally came to a stack of envelopes bound by two rubber bands that contained photos of the top floor rooms and hallway where Jill had been taken, bound, and gagged. Removing the rubber bands and opening the top envelope, I pulled out a set of photos depicting the hallway. I saw that absent from all views was any evidence of cameras.

This hallway, on the top floor of the building, was markedly different from the rest, with artwork adorning the corridor, hardwood floors with throw rugs in the alcoves, and small chandeliers running the length of the hall. *This is where the one-percenters stay*, I thought to myself.

The photos, as they worked their way down the hallway, showed the elevator. There was only one elevator servicing this floor and, as I understood, it required a special card to access.

In my notes, I wrote, 'Could rooms on this floor be reserved for the public', and 'cost?' It was obviously exclusive, but if it were a public space, why were there no cameras on this floor, as there were on all the others?

The next photo in the stack was a vending area marked "Hiding spot – Justin," which must have been the place Justin ducked into after he had encountered his manager accompanied by the thugs. I knew this from the briefing Janet had provided.

Moving on, I saw a photo of the door of the utility closet used by housekeeping, and then a photo of the inside, marked 'location of second incident.' *Incident*, I thought, wanting to punch something. This *incident* would stay with this young woman for the rest of her life. I could only imagine the fear she must have experienced. It only served to further my determination.

The last set of photos showed the hallway, door, and room where the party had occurred, and the direction from which the manager and two thugs had approached Justin.

I took another sip of coffee, settled myself to the task at hand, and set the photos aside.

Closing my eyes to process all that I had seen, it hit me like a lightning bolt. My heart racing, I went back to the stack of photos showing the grounds and common areas.

There it is!

I ripped open the envelope marked 'video footage' and found a flash drive tucked inside. I slid it into my laptop and hit play. I was looking for one thing this time, and one thing only.

I found what I was looking for on the video footage of the pool area.

My heart pounded faster. From the viewpoint of a camera perched atop the tiki hut bar, I could just make out a profile of the man I had unceremoniously nicknamed 'Shrek', before he, and the manager who had abducted Jill, turned away and moved just out of camera range where their forms blurred. They must have known about the location and range of this camera and wanted to steer clear.

I reversed the tape to the only clear image of them and paused it. What I saw turned me cold inside.

They were looking toward Jill as she sunbathed on the lounge chair. It could have been my imagination, but the look that Shrek gave was frightful. I reversed the tape several times and caught, in one short frame, a glance from Shrek to a man in a lounge chair toward the end of the row. He bore the presence of someone with money — and lots of it.

When I froze the only decent image of him, before he stood up and moved out of the picture, I could see that he wore what looked to be expensive sunglasses, and an unbuttoned Hawaiian shirt that revealed a large gold chain holding a medallion of some sort. I could also see the glint of gold from a ring on his hand.

I screen-shot the image, wondering if this might be the man behind the curtain of the criminal enterprise. I couldn't wait to share this information with Janet.

Stifling a rising tide of excitement, I decided to set these thoughts aside for the time being and get back to work on the issues pertinent to my role as an expert on hospitality and entertainment safety.

I looked next at the report from the expert witness for the defense on hospitality safety. The defense expert opined in his report that there was no law or rule mandating the use of cameras in hotel hallways or elevators, and gave the opinion that having cameras in the hallways and elevators, while not an invasion of privacy, was inconsiderate to guests and made them feel uncomfortable — as though they were always under the watchful eye of 'big brother'.

"Hmmm," I murmured to myself. This expert seemed to be moving into an area of opinion that would not serve them well at trial.

I agreed that there were no laws or rules mandating cameras in hotel hallways — at least none of which I was aware, and certainly none in this State. It was, however, in my opinion, very good practice to have cameras from the standpoint of safety. I was aware of several cases where people were assaulted in hotel rooms.

Cameras not only acted as good devices for providing evidence when an assault, theft, — or worse – occurred, but also acted as a deterrent to unlawful and criminal behaviors. I also knew that not all hotels had cameras, but it was certainly not uncommon for hotels to have cameras mounted in hallways, the front desk area, and other common areas.

I knew from experience that some theme parks had cameras placed at strategic locations throughout the entire park, often hiding them in nooks and crannies, or concealed in other clever ways. It was good policy, in my opinion, for guest safety, and for use as evidence if guests sued — a frequent occurrence in our litigious society.

I made notes that would serve as reminders for key points I would use in my response to this report.

Reading further, I saw where their expert said that it was not standard practice for hotels to have cameras in public areas, and *could* not in private areas. This got to the heart of this expert's opinion — that the top floor was not a public area, as it was reserved only for the small number of guests who used and frequented this floor.

The argument was, as I now understood from the report — that the *entire* top floor — including the hallway, was viewed as a place where there was an expectation of privacy. The report even mentioned that guests would often leave their doors open, and walk down the hallways clad only in their bathrobes, or less. *TMI*, I thought to myself.

My report would need to address this issue since, in my experience, and from my teaching and research on the subject, it was clear that there was an expectation of privacy in guest rooms, locker/changing rooms, and bathrooms, but I had never seen hotel hallways considered an area of a hotel where there was an expectation of privacy.

People could open the doors to their rooms, and walk the hallways in their bathrobes if they wanted, but this didn't trigger an expectation of privacy. In other words, the actions of the hotel guests did not create an expectation of privacy in a public space. Also, the top floor was not a private residence or dwelling. Heck, if I won the lottery, I could reserve a room up there. I was keen to address this issue in my report.

The expert for the defense went on to talk about how, while the manager was certainly at fault for his actions, the organizational structure of the organization, as with most resorts, granted substantial authority and independence to management. This allowed management to employ creative thinking to solve problems and move rapidly in resolving issues.

OK, I thought. *Way to pass the buck.* The ability to work independently without undue interference from upper management was often a good thing, and it did often promote creativity and efficiency, but balance was the key.

A key aspect of upper management's job, in recreation and hospitality settings, was to ensure that policies and procedures were followed — particularly those essential to safety. They were therefore responsible for the actions of resort hotel managers, those responsible for carrying out safety protocols. This was a key tenet of the doctrine of respondeat superior. It was both irresponsible and incorrect, in my opinion, to say that upper management could turn a blind eye and wipe its hands of the actions of their employees. This whole situation was case in point.

Reading further, the expert for the defense went on to address the background of the manager and the resort's hiring practices — a key claim made by the plaintiffs in the negligence claim. He said that although the manager, Johnny Grubbs, had a previous misdemeanor on his record for possession of marijuana, and a complaint of sexual harassment that never resulted in a guilty verdict, his record was otherwise clean at the time of hire — and failed to rise to a level, in their opinion, that warranted reasonable concerns on the background check. Also, once hired, upper management claimed to have no knowledge of his personal indiscretions, and immediately fired him once it came to their attention that he was involved in human trafficking.

Personal indiscretions, I'll say, I thought, with disgust.

The background check also failed, in the expert's opinion, to raise any red flags about potential kidnapping, sex trafficking, or abduction propensities, the issue in the present case. His actions, he opined, were completely unforeseeable to the ordinary person, as well as the upper management of the resort.

I would need to dig into Grubb's background a bit more, particularly since I had now seen him with Shrek. There had to be *something* that the background check had missed. You didn't become a monster like Grubbs overnight.

Paging through the files, I found one labeled 'Employee background checks — policy'. Reading through the documents, I discovered that the resort policy on background checks only required a criminal background check for crimes committed *within* the state. *There's a good chance*, I thought to myself, *that Grubbs had committed crimes in other states.*

I would need to speak with Janet about this. You didn't just jump from one misdemeanor to full-out felony kidnapping and human trafficking. It just didn't make sense, and when things didn't add up — I had learned from experience — there was usually a reason.

I finished reading the report and spent the remainder of the day reading through the stacks of case materials. It was after five before I finished reading the last of them. I built a roaring fire, made a nice dinner, and settled back to allow my mind to process the information it had absorbed.

With thoughts of the case still swirling through my mind, I drifted into a deep sleep, with facts and objective reasoning replaced with ghastly, otherworldly images of armed assailants chasing me down streets and through alleyways.

A restful night of sleep eluded me.

CHAPTER 15

At 9:30 the following morning, I called the number Janet had left for me — handwritten on the top page of the first stack of case materials. On this page was a list of numbers, with instructions to only call each number once from my burner phone.

I dialed the first one on the list, and Janet wasted no time answering.

"Hi Dr. Strickland. Thank God. It is good to hear from you," she said between breaths. "Harvey, my paralegal, and the man you met at the exchange told us you all had a very close scrape."

"How is he?" I asked, of the man whose name I now knew.

"Harvey is fine. It is *you* I'm worried about. He told me that a pickup truck almost ran you down, and that you narrowly escaped a trap they had laid for you. He was watching it all unfold and told me about your amazing bike handling skills."

"I was just lucky, I guess," I said with modesty.

"Seemed like more than luck to me," said Janet. "Harvey called 911, but by the time the police had arrived, your attackers in the pickup trucks had scattered. He couldn't get a license plate number, but said he had a decent look at the trucks and identified the make and models."

"That's a step in the right direction," I added. "I was able to get a good look at some of their faces. One is the same man who threatened me on the courthouse steps."

"I'll provide this information to law enforcement, and I'm sure they would like for you to give descriptions so they can draw sketches and send out a BOLO for these guys."

"I'd be more than happy to make a statement, but would like to do it remotely if possible. I'm not in the mood to travel right now, if you know what I mean."

"I understand," said Janet. "We will work with the authorities to set this up. They can take a statement through us, and we can even have a sketch artist come to our firm to work with you remotely."

"OK, just let me know."

"We will, and there is something else you need to know."

Oh boy, I thought. I wasn't sure if I could take any more bad news.

"When the FBI was combing through the burned remains of your condo, they found your cell phone."

"Was it unharmed?" I asked, hoping for some good news.

"No, it was badly damaged… but they *were* able to pull a few incoming text messages from it. One was from your teaching assistant asking about his tasks for the upcoming weeks. But the one of interest came from an anonymous source. It was time-stamped only minutes before your condo was torched. The FBI tried to trace its source but came up empty."

"OK," I replied, my mind numb from the bad news that just wouldn't seem to stop.

"I'll read it to you if you would like, but be warned, it is disturbing."

I took a deep breath and said, "Tell me what it said. I need to know."

"The message read, 'Dr. Strickland, it was so good to meet you earlier today. Despite your rude comment, I like you. I also admire your courage. That is why it saddens me to inform you that my employer believes you represent a threat to his organization and must be eliminated. Please take care — and accept my sincerest apologies'."

My stomach clenched and bile rose in my throat. So, I thought, we now know the torching of my condo was no accident, and it wasn't just meant to scare me. If I had been there and come running out, I'm sure my fate would have been the same as if I had burned to death — I would have been killed either way.

The seconds ticked by as I gathered my composure — and thoughts.

"They tried to kill me twice then," I said in a whisper when I finally spoke.

"Yes, it appears that way," said Janet, in a no-nonsense, matter-of-fact voice.

Oddly, the straight-forward nature of her answer both comforted and disturbed me.

"Are we OK to continue and talk about the case?" she asked.

I suspected she did not intend to be inconsiderate, but to get to the matter at hand, and my role in the case, so I simply replied, "Yes."

"Did you have a chance to review the case materials?"

"Yes," I replied. "I have reviewed all the documents."

"What are your thoughts, especially as it pertains to the report written by the hospitality safety expert for the defense?"

When I had finished providing a synopsis of my reaction to the causes of action, or claims made in the larger lawsuit, I focused on issues that had garnered my attention.

"I saw where the expert for the defense supported an argument, perhaps fed to him by the defense attorneys, that the top floor was a private suite, therefore triggering an expectation of privacy. I don't believe that the top floor was private since anyone with enough money could stay there. I have never seen where this was the case at any other resort. All hallways are, in my opinion, public spaces where cameras could — and should — be mounted for safety reasons."

"Good," said Janet. That will be an important aspect of your testimony. "Can you elaborate on the use of cameras in public spaces?"

"Yes. I have seen them in a fair number of hotels I have inspected for various insurance companies. They are typically located in hallways, and sometimes also in elevators where they may be hidden behind mirrored walls."

"Do you think it is the industry standard?" asked Janet.

"I would say that it is a common practice in the industry to have cameras — video only — in most public spaces such as front desk areas, restaurants, pools, and places like that. This would include hallways and, in some cases, elevators. This hotel had them in hallways and public spaces, all except the top floor where the abduction occurred."

"Good," said Janet. "That is helpful."

"There is something else," I said, my voice laced with anxiety.

"What is that?" asked Janet, a noticeable curiosity in her voice.

"I studied the photos and tapes and saw something interesting. I first saw it in the photo by the pool — the man from the courthouse whom I have sarcastically named 'Shrek,' and the manager, Grubbs, looking toward Jill while she was sitting in the lounge chair."

Janet's voice raised a notch. "Interesting."

"You mentioned the tapes. What else did you find?"

"Shrek and the manager are clearly visible, but only for a second. Before they move out of range, you can see them look from Jill to a man in a lounge chair at the far end of the row. It appears that he gives them a very brief thumbs up."

"I'll need to look at that tape again," said Janet. "We will likely need to share the tape and photos with the FBI. Good work Dr. Strickland. For now, however, please keep this to yourself as we don't want to impede a criminal investigation. I'll take it from here. Now, let's get back to your opinion on the matter for which you have been retained."

"OK," I replied, realizing that I was taking the case a bit too personally. Janet, I had to admit, was right in steering me back to the center. I couldn't fault her for that. But still...

I composed myself, and shifted back to providing my opinion on resort safety. "I also had thoughts on the background check. The defendant's expert, in their report, said that the background check was done correctly, and that a misdemeanor was not enough to trigger concerns about job ability, performance, or safety. Grubbs had one misdemeanor, as stated in the report, for possession of marijuana. I wondered, however, whether the background check was just for this state, or was it national in scope?"

"That is another good catch, and a good question. This was brought up among co-counsel earlier and we investigated it. It seems the resort only relied on data from the state. They did not run a national background check. We are running one now, and should have the results soon. I'll keep you posted. Given his possible association with this man you call 'Shrek,' there are likely more skeletons in his closet. Your testimony on the 'background check' issue may have gained importance."

After discussing a few additional points from the report and my anticipated response, the conversation shifted.

"Dr. Strickland," Janet said, her voice smooth, "we couldn't be more appreciative of your help with the case — all in light of very strange and dangerous circumstances."

"Have you, or any members of your firm been threatened?" I couldn't help but ask.

"Yes, we have, but only recently," said Janet, after a moment's hesitation. "Both me and several of my colleagues who are working on the case — and of course, Harvey, who you so heroically saved from harm. But it isn't the first time, and certainly won't be the last," she said with more confidence.

"I hope that the family finds justice and nails these criminals in the process."

"So do I," said Janet, as she ended the call.

With my mind now fully engaged in the case, I read through the pertinent parts of the case materials again and wrote a draft report summarizing my opinion.

Later, having reached the limits of my endurance on that front and, as the morning turned to afternoon, I made a pot of tea and sat down on the couch with a cup. Staring at the bright yellow, flickering flames in the fireplace, my mind wandered before resting on an idea. It was distant at first, but just like a spark that would burst into flame, it grew until it consumed me. The result was a firm decision — one that I could not escape.

Although it was risky, and I had already been to the resort to inspect the slide and pool area, I hadn't yet been to the elevator and top floor where the stages of abduction took place. I needed to put my feet on the ground and see the elevator and top floor where the abduction occurred — if I could even get access. It was also reasonable, I assumed, to believe that Shrek and his cohorts would be long gone — and this would be the last place they would attempt to look for me.

After a late lunch, followed by an hour of meditation and a long walk along the river trail, I was ready for my clandestine visit to the resort.

It was time to roll.

CHAPTER 16

Back at the garage, I looked across the spotless room and spied the Bentley and Porsche Cayenne. I mentally flipped a coin for which car to take and came up with the Cayenne. It was classy, fast, and powerful, and would blend in well with the other luxury vehicles that were sure to be parked at the resort.

I glided along the freeway in the direction of the resort, experiencing the freedom that only came from movement — and the exhilaration of driving a vehicle like the Porsche Cayenne. As was customary these days, I diligently checked my rearview mirrors for any signs that someone might be following me, and eventually made my way to the front entrance of the resort.

Passing to the right of the guard shack, I followed closely behind a guest with a room key who had just swiped his card to raise the arm of the bar, and shot through in his wake, looking like an impatient and entitled rich hotel guest who was late for a dinner appointment. The guard didn't even glance in my direction.

Little did I know, however, that the unblinking eye of the unobtrusive camera on the roof of the guard shack recorded everything. I was happily oblivious.

I entered the parking lot, found a parking space, and made my way to the front entrance. I was met with a charming but slightly intimidating sight — large, quarried granite stones framing a grand entranceway, with koi ponds and native flora and fauna lining the walkway — meant to both awe and calm guests upon arrival. The centerpiece was a large, bronze sculpture of a wolf, standing majestically atop a stone mound. Upon entering through the sliding glass doors, I understood the complexity and scope of the building and grounds. The front desk area was adorned in dark mahogany, beyond which were hallways to the left and right.

I had no way to know which hallway led to the elevators leading to the top floor, but knew that Jill had left the pool to make her way back to her room on the fourteenth floor when she had been abducted. She may have been fooled by the manager into thinking that the elevator she had taken would lead her back to her floor.

The pool would be my starting point.

After a few wrong turns and retracing steps, I finally arrived. A quick look, and I could see that this was way more than just your ordinary pool. It was more like a waterpark. "What should I do now?" I asked myself, feeling very much out of place. I was, at least, dressed for the part, wearing a brightly colored sundress, and sandals. "Well, when in Rome…" I said softly, as a thought came to me. It was time to visit the tiki bar.

I set a course in that direction, weaving around lounging guests who were soaking up the last good rays of sunlight, arriving at last to the bar.

I had just walked up, when a kindly older lady with wrinkles framing intelligent eyes, asked, "What will it be, dear?"

"I'd like a virgin Mojito, please."

"Coming right up, honey."

While I was waiting for my drink, I looked across the pool — from the vantage of the camera I knew sat atop the tiki hut — and scanned the pool chairs that lined the side of the pool opposite from me. It would ordinarily provide a sense of excitement to be at a fancy resort, but knowing what had transpired here, it only left me with a sense of dread.

Monsters had lurked here, and innocence had been lost.

Noticing the look on my face, the bartender asked, "Honey, are you OK? It looks like you've seen a ghost."

"Oh no, I'm fine, thank you," I lied, taking the drink, and heading in the direction most likely to provide access to the top floor.

I took a deep drink of the cool, delicious liquid, hoping that it would settle my nerves. It tasted good but didn't help ease the crushing sense of anxiety. I continued walking.

The alcove was just ahead, the most likely place that Jill had gone as she had attempted to make her way back to the room. As I approached, I could just make out two elevators standing side by side. Standing in front of them, I noticed both a card pad and push button.

So, this must be how it worked — regular hotel guests would push the button, but the only door that would open for them would be the elevator to the left. The one to the right could only be accessed with a card key. Good money said that the elevator on the right went to the top floor.

It looked as though I had reached a dead end. *I need to come back later with a better plan,* I thought to myself, as the afternoon was quickly transitioning to evening. It was then that a polite and wealthy-looking man approached.

As he waved his card key against the reader as if it were a credit card he was using for purchase, I saw an opportunity.

The man smelled of expensive cologne and was dressed in the type of clothing designed to help rich people fit in — a loose-fitting shirt and jeans, with discrete labels from top of the line clothiers. The Hermes sandals were an added touch. Still, there was something about the man that was unrefined, and perhaps even dangerous.

In my most confident voice and feigning arrogance, I asked, "Mind if I join you? I left my key in the room."

My heart was pounding so hard I could feel the pulsing in my temples.

The man slowly looked my way, and with elevator eyes that at once disgusted me and sent a chill down my spine, looked down, and then back up my body until settling on my face. He seemed to have a made a decision.

Looking directly in my eyes, as if trying to read my thoughts, he gave a fake half smile and said, in a voice that made me feel insignificant, "Oh, yes, sure, of course."

The elevator began its nonstop journey to the top floor as alarm bells rang inside my head, and my flight response went into full gear. I now knew how horses must feel when trapped in a burning barn, with the instinct to run nearly leading them to insanity.

It was around the 7th floor, I think, as the elevator made its way upward, that I knew something wasn't right. The only passenger sharing the ride with me pressed an unmarked silver button on the panel to the right of the elevator door and the machine lurched to a stop.

The man then looked at me and I saw his demeanor change — his look of entitled arrogance melted away, to be replaced by an expression that was at once, sinister and treacherous.

"What are you doing?" I asked, through a herculean effort to keep my composure and not betray the fear coursing through me.

His response shocked me to the core.

"Why, we are stopping of course, Dr. Strickland."

"How do you know my name?" I asked, my voice raising a few octaves.

He ignored my question and pulled out a Sig Sauer. The lethal gun was pointed at my chest. Close range, center mass, the man wouldn't miss.

"Dr. Strickland, would you please place your drink on the floor, and then turn around and face away from me."

It was a command in the form of a question which my brain quickly processed, searching for alternatives that all ended in unfavorable outcomes.

I decided to comply. As I turned away, a split second of confusion enveloped me before I passed out, the butt of his gun having collided with my skull, the concussion rendering me unconscious.

When the elevator reached the top floor, my captor was joined by another thug, who dragged my limp body down the hall, my shirt catching on the hardwood floor, threatening to pull it from my body. Exposed skin, I would learn later, had rubbed across the hard surface, leaving patches of angry, red friction burns across my back.

I was pulled into a luxury suite, one that was not purposed for my leisure on this particular night. As it turned out, it was the same one that Jill, alone and afraid, had been taken to not long ago.

The goons bound and gagged me with duct tape and zip ties — the tools of the trade for most kidnappers. I was dropped on the couch in the main room, where I would remain — my fate in the hands of dangerous men — until I awoke with a pounding head, and a feeling of fear and helplessness that was as debilitating as the bonds that held me.

At some point before I woke from my involuntary, dreamless state, I heard, as if in a dark cave, a barely discernable conservation.

"Yes sir," said the voice, as he spoke nervously into his cell phone. "We have Dr. Strickland in our possession. It was indeed an opportunity that we couldn't pass up. What would you like for us to do with her?" After a moment, the distant voice said, "Yes sir. We will do as instructed."

Then the world went silent once again.

Sometime later, I regained consciousness, feeling slightly nauseous and dizzy. I had seen enough crime shows to know that it was wise to not show your hand, and so I laid there with my eyes closed, listening for any sounds from my captors.

The room was silent — and not just silent from someone trying to keep quiet. It was the type of silence where you knew in your gut that you were alone. Still, I didn't move for a full five minutes, my ears tuned to the slightest sound.

When I was confident that I was alone, I peeked through narrowed lids to see where they were holding me.

It looked, by all appearances, to be a hotel guest room — some type of suite. I made out chairs and a television and determined that I was lying on a couch with my hands and feet zip tied. Moving my lips slightly, I felt the sticky and confining sensation of tape — most likely duct tape.

What I didn't see was people. While this gave me some comfort, it also speared a sense of urgency through me. *How long do I have before they come back? This might be my only chance of escape.*

I noticed that the zip ties were just loose enough to wiggle my hands free. Rising to remove the tape from my mouth, and free my ankles, a wave of pain and dizziness fell over me — enough to lay me back down on the couch. The clock was ticking, and the window of escape was tight, so I willed myself back to a sitting position and freed my bonds.

Standing, I gained my balance and took in the surroundings. The room was neat and orderly. It was also clean. In fact, it was abnormally clean. The only evidence that the room had been occupied by anyone other than me was a piece of hotel stationery on the couch's end table. Despite my hurry, I picked up the paper to read what it said. The words filled me with horror.

'Antonio, I have left to attend to other matters for the syndicate in LA. My flight leaves within the hour. The boss left me with instructions. When you arrive, you are free to show the woman whatever level of companionship you wish. Then you may wash your hands of her. Please sanitize the room afterwards. As usual, leave no forensic evidence.'

Angry and fearing for my life, I crammed the paper into my pocket and headed toward the door. Throwing caution to the wind, and with an unquenchable urge to run, I threw the door open and raced down the hallway in the direction of the emergency stairway. Entering the stairs, I heard the door close and lock behind me. I spied a fire alarm and pulled it, then ran down the stairs, my legs burning in pain. When I reached the bottom floor, I burst through the exit door and into the parking lot, my head pounding from the exertion. It appeared that I was alone, but I dared not delay. Spotting the

Porsche two lots over, I ran with all my might toward the safety it promised.

Several people saw me running, looks of confusion and worry crossing their faces. With my mind racing and head pounding, I didn't know whether they were friend or foe, so I just continued to move with a single-minded purpose — to get as far away from the resort as possible. Reaching the relative safety of my vehicle, I started the ignition, and the Porsche roared to life. The safety and comfort of the vehicle helped to slow my breathing and steady my mind.

I drove cautiously back to the main road and toward the safety of the cabin, taking side roads, and random turns, to be certain that I wasn't followed.

CHAPTER 17

I returned the Porsche to its place in the garage and, leaving the keys on the seat, stepped into the brightly lit space and made my way to the door. I was badly shaken, and my primal instincts had seized control — warning me to stay near the light, and away from the darkness that awaited outside. Through an extreme act of will, I used logic and reason to convince my legs to move — that the threat was miles away back at the resort, not here at this place.

Reason won the day, and I stepped out into the darkness of early night. As I stood in the dark, giving my eyes a minute to adjust and gain my bearings, I was overwhelmed by the feeling that danger lurked behind every bush and tree. I ran harder than I ever remember, toward the safety of the cabin as chills raced up my spine in uncontrollable waves.

When I reached the cabin, I pushed back the instinctual fear of what lay outside to ensure that the cabin, my primary place of refuge, was secure. I inspected the outside of the cabin, only entering after making sure that all the doors and windows were secure.

I then entered and locked the door behind me, to the comforting "beep, beep" of the alarm system. Next, I entered the code to disarm it, only to immediately re-enter the code to arm it again. I wasn't sure if it would matter given what I was up against, but it didn't hurt — and I needed the assurance.

It was late, but I desperately wanted to talk with someone — a person who shared a stake in the dangerous game that was playing out. I was holding a cold soda pulled from the fridge, and noticed that my hand was shaking. It seemed my world had been turned upside down, and then, for good measure, spun every which way — leaving me completely ungrounded.

With the writing desk in my sights, I walked to it, and pulled the top sheet from a stack of papers within easy reach. On it was the list of burner numbers that Janet had written. My eyes scanned the sheet, seeing that I had marked through the top number. I moved to the next, then dialed and waited. As the ringing sound moved past the point my mind perceived as pointless to continue, a groggy voice said, "Dr. Strickland, is that you? Is everything alright?"

In a rush of words, I told her, without preamble, all that had transpired earlier, from the time I had arrived at the resort to my arrival back at the cabin. I told her about the note, and the reference to a crime syndicate out of LA, presumably very large in scope.

My story must have fully awoken her, as her voice suddenly became crisp and clear. She said, "I'm glad you are OK. It wasn't wise to do what you did. From now on, please consult me first, before going on any more ill-advised adventures."

"OK," I said, quietly, disappointed to not receive the level of sympathy that I sought. "I just needed to see some things for myself."

"And it seems that it almost got you killed," said Janet, with heat in her voice.

"Well, I'm not so sure," I replied, as a thought, one that had been lurking just outside my consciousness, occurred to me. "Remember how I told you they bound and gagged me? After I had regained consciousness, I remember now that the zip ties weren't all that tight. Tight enough to make me think they intended to bind my wrists and ankles, but loose enough to allow me to escape. And why not just kill me while I was unconscious? It would have been more efficient."

My words seemed to be coming from someone else, looking down at the situation from a safe distance. I tried to keep my mind thinking objectively for fear that making it personal would crush me under the weight of my words.

Janet remained silent and allowed me to continue.

"And the note — I wonder if it was staged."

Was I just being paranoid? Those of us in academia often had a laundry list of nagging fears. Would we be promoted and tenured, or would someone torpedo our career? Would our academic programs be sun-set due to lack of interest or funding? There were also so many ways that our ambitious and unethical colleagues might marginalize or destroy us.

I was always looking over my shoulder, and the first to admit that paranoia had become a part of my everyday life. I had to ask myself whether my current thoughts were just the product of a paranoid mind, or whether they had merit.

Janet's response was slightly reassuring. "Dr. Strickland, I think you make a good point. We should certainly investigate this angle. We cannot, however, rule out the possibility that these goons, part of some large criminal enterprise based in LA, *did* intend to kill you and will be coming after you again. Are you sure that you weren't followed?"

"Yes," I replied confidently.

"Then you should be safe. Also, given the random nature of the incident, they probably didn't have the opportunity to place a tracking device on your vehicle. You might still want to check under the vehicle, regardless. Better to be safe than sorry.”

There was that word again — “Incident.” It gave me pause, but I shrugged it off. I knew from experience that Janet was an objective thinker.

“That makes me feel better,” I said, “and I’ll check the car tomorrow when I have a chance. It never hurts to be overly careful. I would be a bit too creeped out to walk over there in the dark tonight though, given what just happened.”

“That makes sense,” said Janet. “And since the FBI will need a copy of that message, and it is too risky to send by email from your computer, can you read it to me again. I’ll write it down and make a copy to share with them. I’ll also let them know where the abduction occurred so they can bring in a forensics team and investigate. For now, I would suggest that you keep this between us and lie low.”

I read the note back to Janet slowly, and when she had copied the words, I pleaded, “Please let me know what they find.”

“I will,” said Janet, all serious and lawyer-like.

“I can’t thank you enough.”

“I think it should be the other way around,” said Janet, “but you are welcome.”

As the call ended and the phone went silent, a crushing feeling of loneliness was added to helplessness and fear.

I laid down on the couch with the lights on, and fell into a deep sleep, dreaming that I was at a waterpark, soaking in the sun, and reveling in the sights and sounds of children and their families laughing and playing. Shifting suddenly, the pleasant dream became a nightmare as the sky turned dark and tornadoes ripped through the park, grabbing everyone and everything in its path.

Standing apart, as a spectator in the dream, I watched until the cries and screams of parents and children faded as the whirling winds carried everyone away, leaving nothing but a single sheet of paper with something written on it. I walked through puddles of water in a barren, gray landscape, and picked up the paper. The words, "You've been played," were written in dark red ink that bled through the paper.

I awoke with a start, and noticed that the first rays of sunlight from the new day were casting a warm glow inside the cabin. My mind struggled to separate the dream from reality, and then return to the memory of the dream. I recalled the nightmare and then, the words on the paper, boldly confronting me — "You've been played."

My subconscious mind was telling the part of my brain that dealt with the zillion daily realities that confronted it, that there was something it should know.

The next hour was spent analyzing the circumstances of my abduction from every angle, and reading the note, over and over, until it was burned into my memory and merged within the larger context.

Like a computer program that takes multiple data points and spits out a solution, my mind reached its own: *I had indeed been played.* It was an elaborate ruse, and a smart one.

I now felt certain that the people behind my abduction, and most likely Jill's, were trying to mislead me — *but to what end? And who is behind it all?*

I needed coffee and a bite to eat.

With sustenance in hand, I moved to the desk, where my trusted computer was sitting, and fired it up. I had decided to set the overpowering thoughts of my recent experience aside for now, and focus on something that would center me — so I pulled up my next lecture and began working.

I would need to remain in hiding until the trial. That was a no-brainer. That would mean that Andy would have to teach my class for at least several more weeks and would need more lecture material.

I set to work, opening the metaphorical door to the closet in my mind, heaping all the traumatic thoughts and fears into it — then shutting and locking the door on those thoughts.

Trouble would find me soon enough. Of that, I was certain. In fact, it was probably knocking on the door even now, despite my attempt to will thoughts of it from my mind.

CHAPTER 18

The next topic on the syllabus is waivers. This is a topic I enjoy teaching, as it holds implications for managing risk, and gives me the opportunity to introduce my students to contract law, since a waiver is a type of contract.

I know that most of my students will deal with waivers as managers, and not as lawyers. A few of my students go on to work in the legal profession, but my courses are designed for managers to gain a basic understanding of the legal and safety issues they will face in the profession. As such, they will be the ones who work with attorneys to point out the unique hazards and safety issues faced in the venues they manage. They will also be responsible for distributing waivers to their guests and assuring they are administered properly.

I recall a case where I served as a legal consultant to the defense in a motocross accident on private land. Having been hired by the defense, they asked me to conduct a site inspection. It was a bright sunny day when I arrived at the two-hundred-acre property owned by a crusty old-timer named Ron. He met me at the gate to his property, which he opened to the public for motocross events and recreational activities, in an old Ford pickup truck.

The lead attorney on the case had told me to come out early to get started on the inspection of the premises. She had a deposition that morning and would meet me at the property when it was finished. Sitting in my SUV, upon my arrival, at the entrance to a long dirt road, I watched Ron step out of his truck along with a rangy old blue tick hound, and unlock and open the gate. He returned to his truck and started back up the road, just expecting I would follow.

When we reached a weathered gatehouse, he pulled to the side, dust billowing up behind him, and waved for me to pull over as well. I grabbed my stuff, shut the door behind me and, doing as summoned, walked over to his truck. He smiled and said, "Hop on in. I hope you like dogs."

Fortunately, dogs had been a big part of my life for a long time — all of it, actually — until I moved into my condo. *I would need to get another dog as soon as I had a place with a yard*, I mused.

With Ron at the wheel, the hound perched happily in the center, and me by the window, we set off to inspect the site of the accident. I had been told by the attorney that a young man of eighteen years had been riding his off-road motocross motorcycle on one of the trails when he lost control while rounding a curve in the path, his bike careening off the trail and colliding with a large sycamore tree. He had suffered severe injuries — a broken neck, crushed pelvis, and multiple internal injuries. Although he survived, he would suffer from these devastating, lifelong injuries.

The plaintiff attorneys clearly smelled a big payday.

I inspected the site of the crash, and tried to make sense of it. As an experienced off-road cyclist, I realized it didn't add up. Ron told me he understood the man was experienced, was not under the influence of drugs or alcohol, and was riding on a day as clear as this one. I observed the area, and noted that the turn in the path was clearly visible from at least 50 yards away, and was free of debris, roots, or other obstructions.

I asked about warning and safety signage and Ron told me that there was a sign at the gatehouse with rules on alcohol and rowdy behavior, but no safety warnings there or in the park itself — the area where people would camp and ride. He then pulled out an old, crumpled piece of paper, smoothed it in on the hood of the car, and handed it to me.

It was the waiver he provided to guests of the property, and which they were required to sign when entering the "park." I knew a waiver was a contract, a point that I stressed to my students, and presented on my opening PowerPoint slide.

Contract law had its fair share of complex issues, so many in fact, that law students spent at least a whole semester in law school learning the intricacies of this area of law. For managers, who needed a more practical perspective, however, it is best to provide just that — *a practical perspective,* and one covered in much less detail.

The basic premise, and key requirement for valid contracts, is that — usually a buyer, but for waivers, the patron or guest — understands the terms of the contract. In other words, they need to know what they agree to.

The words at the top of the crumpled piece of paper that Ron was using as a waiver said, 'Contract of Indemnification.' OK, that was all well and good if you were a lawyer, but for most people, this didn't mean squat. While it likely didn't invalidate the waiver, it would have been best if Ron had just called it what most people understand — a "Waiver."

The old blue tick hound had lost interest and ran off chasing a rabbit.

Reading through the document, I also saw a lot of legalese — "heretofores," "wheretofores," and complex legal terminology — which may sound fancy and impressive but does little to help the average person understand what they are reading. Just looking at the page, I had to squint, since most of the text was in small font. It was hard to read. While not invalidating the contract, I believed it might provide an "out" for a plaintiff who wished to argue that they didn't understand what they were getting into.

I don't think that Ron had worked with an attorney on the waiver, as it looked like he had just found a template — and a bad one at that — and filled in the blanks. It read mostly like a list of rules to follow, and consequences if they weren't followed. It also had some blanket waiver language, saying that the park was immune from "all liabilities whatsoever."

I knew some courts frowned upon this type of broad language, preferring that waivers be more specific in the negligent actions to which they offered protection from liability. It was the same for the term "gross negligence," one that was used in the waiver. Most courts frowned on providing protection from liability where the defendant did something that was extremely careless.

At least, as Ron had told me, the young man who was injured was not intoxicated, and had the "legal capacity" to sign and understand the contract due to his age and the fact that he wasn't mentally incompetent.

That was about the only bright spot, as the waiver neglected to list the specific risks involved in motocross. Waivers, I would tell my students, might, when well-written, help a defendant raise the defense of assumption of risk — a defense of negligence. To assume a risk, a person needs to know what they are getting into — what the risks of the activity entail — and voluntarily participate when knowing those risks. You couldn't tell from the waiver, as I recalled, what the risks were — and I knew there were plenty when people were racing around unfamiliar, unimproved trails on dirt bikes.

Later, as I would learn from my attorney, the defense had decided not to use the waiver in their defense. It was too poorly written. Also, absent any documentation warning of the types of risks one might encounter while riding in the park, or warning signage, the case, it had been decided, was too difficult to defend and take to trial in front of a jury. They were prepared to pay out a large sum to the plaintiff.

As they prepared to settle the case, a thought came to me. I just couldn't shake the question of how a sober, experienced motocross biker could have made such a serious miscalculation in broad daylight. I had ridden for years and I could have made the turn with ease.

Could there have been another factor? Bad weather and alcohol had been ruled out. Then it hit me. One other possibility remained.

Sitting in front of my computer, I had googled the Consumer Product Safety Commission website, a great resource for product safety issues. In addition to providing safety information on many products relevant to my area of study, the CPSC also provided information on product recalls. With fingers crossed, I accessed the recall page and typed in the make and model of the dirt bike the plaintiff had been riding. I then hit 'submit.'

To my satisfaction, the specific bike at issue came up on the site, and bingo! The bike had been recalled due to a defect in the braking system.

The cause of the plaintiff's injury was therefore not the fault of the landowner, but instead the fault of a defective bike. I learned that the plaintiff later sued the business that had sold him the defective bike, learning they knew of the recall but had withheld that information.

It also later came to my attention that Ron had made changes to improve the safety of his park, and had a new and improved waiver. And since Ron would not be sued out of existence, the old hound could continue to enjoy his life of chasing rabbits. It was a win-win-win, and one of the reasons that I loved doing this kind of work.

I typed up notes for Andy, providing a synopsis of my story, along with updated PowerPoint slides, and went to the couch to put my feet up. The shadows outside were growing long and it was getting cooler outside, so I made a drink, lit a fire in the fireplace, and relaxed. The mental exertion had left me feeling good, and was a great diversion from my larger troubles.

The night — and remainder of the week — were uneventful. I had finished my report for Janet on time, providing my opinion as an expert relevant to resort safety in the context of Jill's abduction and mailed it from a rural post office a good twenty miles away. It felt good to have that out of the way.

My life felt almost normal. But that was about to change.

CHAPTER 19

It was one of those gorgeous fall days when the air was clear and the chill just enough to require a fleece or light jacket, but not anything heavier. I was sitting on the porch fine tuning some lectures and reading through the case materials for another case on which I'd been retained. It was a negligence case, where the plaintiff was seeking fifteen million dollars for the "pain and suffering" associated with their injury.

It seemed that every time you turned around, there was another lawsuit. Ever since the 1980s, society had become more and more litigious. Some speculate that it was the loosening of marketing requirements, setting loose a flood of advertisements among services for lawyers. I liked to tell my students about a case that was decided in the late 1970s, *Bates v. State Bar of Arizona*, where an attorney sued for the right to advertise. His argument, based on the First Amendment right to freedom of speech, pointed to numerous other businesses — most all, really — that were allowed to advertise. He prevailed in his suit and from that point forward, advertisements for legal services have seemed to spring up everywhere.

Some have speculated that the enormous number of civil lawsuits — numbering in the many thousands — is driven by the evolution of a lottery mentality and the hope for a big payday, while others believe that the competitive market, or changes in societal values are the culprit. I personally believe that it is a combination of factors, but all too often could be summed up by one word, "greed." For that reason, I only consult on cases that I believe have merit, and where justice would be best served in a victory for an injured plaintiff, or defense of meritless claim.

The number of lawsuits brought in the context of sport, recreation and entertainment seem boundless, with most — somewhere north of ninety percent, I've been told — settling without ever going to trial. This made sense for many defendants in the hospitality industry because trials are usually bad for public relations — families don't want to visit, for example, a theme park they think was unsafe. The discovery and trial process can also be quite stressful, as one can imagine, and sometimes, when appeals are made to the upper courts, cases are drawn out over many years.

I teach a legal issues class for recreation and hospitality managers and love the debates and discussions that ensue when cases are presented in class. Every semester I will bring up the still-famous coffee case where an elderly woman spilled hot coffee in her lap while visiting the drive-through at a fast-food establishment. She suffered severe burns after spilling the extremely hot coffee in her lap, and sued. Although this case happened many years ago, it remains in our collective conscious, and always results in a lively debate.

Wrapped in thought, and over the roar of the river, I almost didn't hear it — the sound of crunching gravel as the SUV approached.

I quickly stuffed my computer into its bag, rose from my seat, and backed along the side of the house, peering around the corner at the front driveway. What I saw sent adrenaline pumping through my veins, preparing my body for immediate action. Doors opened and four men stepped out, each looking deadly serious and carrying snub-nosed automatic weapons. The one in the lead, I noticed to my dismay, was my "good friend" Shrek.

My heart racing, I slung the bag containing my electronic devices over my shoulder and vaulted over the deck railing. Thankfully, the main body of the house concealed my escape

— at least momentarily. As I picked my way through a dense copse of trees, the branches swishing and scraping past, I saw the outline of the old barn, with its hidden secrets.

My options were limited. I can make a run for it — through the forest — but that will likely just extend my freedom for a short period, as they will hunt me down eventually. I can make a run for the Harley, but they will hear the roar of the engine and be on me before I can escape. That leaves only one option — the barn. I will find a place to hide inside, and hope they don't find me.

Running crouched, and picking my way through the trees, I reached the door just as the staccato sound of automatic gunfire raining bullets into the cabin reached my ears.

Boy, some house guest I turned out to be. I am sure that no more invitations will be forthcoming. I have bigger and more immediate worries, though. I need to get the heck out of Dodge before those bullets start coming in my direction.

With these thoughts spurring me on, I unlocked the padlock, pocketed it, stepped inside, and shut the door behind me. There was no opportunity to replace the lock, so I just had to hope they wouldn't notice.

In another moment, I was through the inner door, hearing the soft hiss of it closing behind me. I stood in the open, brightly lit space and questioned whether I had made the right decision. I was certain that by now, they had searched the cabin and found it empty. The next and most logical move would be to inspect the barn.

The clock was ticking.

I looked around the open space, occupied by the wonderful assortment of vehicles. It was immediately clear that I had made a monumentally bad decision. This is not a good place to hide.

The only hiding places that came immediately to mind were a small storage room and bathroom — places they were certain to look. Another option was to jump into one of the SUVs and hide, or start it up and crash through the bay door to escape. Neither of these possibilities held much promise, though, as my mind raced through the possible options. The vehicles will likely be the first place they look, and it is a sure bet they have left at least two of their goons outside the door to cover that avenue of escape. All they have to do is shoot out my tires and it is "game over."

My mind continued to race, weighing the options and probabilities of success — and coming up empty. I had nearly given up all hope when a thought came to me. I had noticed earlier that the garage was not just for show, but also served as a place where the vehicles were maintained, as several had a covered grease pit beneath them.

I ran across the open space to the Bentley, the vehicle with the highest clearance. I looked beneath and saw a handle that was flush with the flooring. I grabbed it and pulled upward; an extremely difficult task given my awkward position. I raised the heavy metal cover just high enough and jammed my foot beneath. Next, I slid sideways, inserting my leg and right hip into the length of the opening. Now on my back, and with better leverage, I pushed upward until the cover met the underside of the Bentley, providing just enough space to slip my body through. Sliding fully through, I landed hard on a short set of steps, while the hatch above me fell back into place with a "clang."

It was pitch black in the pit, which smelled of lubricating oil and gasoline. I struggled to contain a rising panic in the dark and confined space — a place that I hope won't now serve as my coffin.

A moment later I felt, as much as heard, a loud explosion. They must have blown the door. When the ringing in my ears had stopped, the next sound was the heavy footfalls of men wearing boots. As they neared my position, I heard the doors of the Bentley open and close, and someone shout "clear."

I held my breath and remained perfectly still. The urge to open the hatch and flee was overwhelming, but still I waited. I closed my eyes, and concentrated on listening for the sound of movement above me.

At long last, the sounds of activity ceased, and I heard the muffled command of "Let's go. Move it!" Silence then filled the space. It was time to make my move.

CHAPTER 20

This is it, I thought to myself. Either the bad guys had left, or I was a sitting duck. The third possibility didn't hit me until I lifted the lid and smelled smoke, and saw the flickering light of fire.

They had decided to burn the garage to the ground. It seemed they were intent on leaving no stone unturned.

With the world becoming an inferno above me, I could wait no longer.

Choking on smoke, and feeling the searing heat of the fire, I pushed hard on the heavy metal cover, only to have it fall back and entomb me once again. Fear did amazing things to the body. It filled me with a strength I didn't know existed. With all my might, and my remaining strength, I pushed up against the unyielding metal, and this time, won the life and death struggle. With the opportunity presented by the narrow opening, I wedged my arm and shoulder through, and then used the mass of my body to do the rest — wriggling my way through to freedom.

When I gained my feet and looked around, what met my eyes was a scene straight from Dante's Inferno. Orange flames licked the walls, consuming the Ducati and several other precious vehicles. It brought tears to my eyes to see these magnificent machines go up in smoke.

There was no time to dwell on these thoughts though, as I looked back at the door, and around the room — the searing heat of the flames painful to my eyes and skin. There was nowhere to run, as they had poured gasoline throughout the garage, and all avenues of escape were cut off.

The Bentley and I were on a temporary island, which was soon to be consumed by flame. I was clearly now in a state of panic, my mind ruling out all pathways of escape by foot. Then, in a moment of clarity, the obvious solution presented itself.

With seconds to spare, I opened the door to the Bentley and jumped inside. Finding the keys and starting the ignition, I floored the vehicle, racing through the flames and straight for the closed bay door. I only hoped it wasn't strong enough to keep me from busting through.

I kept the pedal to the floor and the superior feat of engineering now under my control responded, hurtling me toward the unknown. The moment before the Bentley crashed into the door, I ducked my head and closed my eyes, an involuntary response to the inevitable collision with a seemingly immovable object.

As it turned out, luck was in my favor, and the Bentley cut through the thin metal door as if it were made of paper. Now outside, with the inferno raging behind me, I quickly sat up and hit the brakes, turning the wheel a moment before colliding with a stand of poplar trees. The Bentley skid to a stop.

I looked around and was relieved to see that I was alone, and not riddled with bullets from the guns of the people who were now so urgently trying to kill me. They must have believed me dead. The thought made me shudder.

To my great dismay, I saw that the fire had now mostly consumed the garage, and those magnificent vehicles along with it. The cabin had been spared the torch, however, which was at least some small consolation. I dreaded telling Laura, even knowing that they could easily have everything replaced, and likely come out even better when it was all said and done.

I backed up and turned down a dirt track road that led off into the woods. I had gone this way on my morning walks and knew that, at least for the few miles that I had walked down, it was passable. I believed it to be an old logging road, and the best direction in which to go, as they may be watching the road leading out — covering all their bases.

The Bentley did a great job of smoothing out the bumps and potholes in the old dirt road and even did an admirable job of fording a small stream that led deep into the woods. Traversing the logging roads far into the woods, I noticed they formed a patchwork of branches. Since I didn't know where I was going anyway, I took random turns that would hopefully throw off any pursuers.

Arriving upon a grassy clearing surrounded by stately old conifers, I pulled to a stop. Night had fallen and there was no sense driving further. This was as good a place as any to spend the night.

I parked the Bentley and set off to gather wood for a fire. It wasn't difficult to find, given all the deadfall in the area, and I was back in short order. Next, I pulled a lighter from the vehicle and started a small fire. You don't see cigarette lighters in cars all that often anymore, but Laura's husband Tony loved good cigars, so had lighters installed in all his vehicles.

I knew that Laura and Tony were freaks when it came to preparation — the perfect scouts — so I opened the back hatch to see if they had any food or other supplies. To my great delight and amazement, it turned out they were well stocked.

A picnic basket held a true bounty — vacuum packed smoked salmon, pasteurized cheese spread, several packages of crackers, a tin of anchovies, assorted nuts, and even packaged cookies and Godiva chocolates. The coup de grâce was a very nice bottle of cabernet. Next to the picnic basket was my next pleasant surprise — sleeping bags, two warm blankets and a pair of pillows. They even had a couple of comfortable fold-out chairs.

It looked like I wouldn't be roughing it tonight, after all.

With a small fire burning, I pulled a chair close to the warmth of the fire and feasted on smoked salmon and crackers while sipping the delicious wine. Somewhere in the trees, an owl hooted, as small critters rustled in the dry leaves beneath.

I was on the run, and feared for my life, but for some reason, in this beautiful slice of untamed land, all alone on a night filled with stars beyond counting, I felt a supreme peace, and not an ounce of fear. The world would keep on turning no matter what happened to me — and that was a comforting thought.

Sitting there, in the vast expanse of wilderness, I looked at my situation, and that of Jill Covington, with a sense of detachment. It was as if this was all an academic exercise, and it was for me alone to solve a complex riddle.

Beneath a blanket of glittering stars, and with a crackling fire in front of me, my mind roamed freely — drifting from thought to thought, but always returning to one. It was Jill's plight, having gained more meaning given my own recent abduction. We now had a shared experience — and I knew the feeling of fear, despair, and anger that she and countless other young women had experienced when abducted and trafficked.

Until now, I could only imagine the horrors and indignities endured by other women as I lived a sheltered life in academia. I recall mentoring a student who aspired to be a lawyer, fighting for the victims of sexual assault on cruise ships. From my experience advising her honors thesis work, I learned that sexual assault on cruise ships was more common than people knew, and jurisdictional issues and challenges in obtaining evidence made these cases very difficult to prosecute. Most ships fly the flags of other countries, and when an assault occurs in international waters, the case often rests within the jurisdiction of the country where the ship is registered.

One can only imagine how difficult it is for a person of average means to hire lawyers and navigate the laws of other countries. Determining jurisdiction, as I tell my students, is an important issue. In the U.S., jurisdiction usually refers to the state where a case is tried. This is very important since the laws in each state are often different, and might go a long way in determining the outcome of a case — in favor of either a plaintiff or defendant. It is, as one might imagine, often very challenging when the laws of different countries are at issue. Then, factor in the time and expense of traveling to another country for trial, and it is daunting to even think about.

And even if the U.S. has jurisdiction, there are often challenges to acquiring evidence — a perpetrator jumps ship in their home port, or the ship lacks rape kits that provide critical evidence. The victim of sexual assault on a cruise ship often faces an Everest-sized challenge.

My student went on to earn her law degree and work as an advocate for victims of sexual assault. I couldn't be prouder of her.

CHAPTER 21

Somewhere deep in the forest, an owl hooted, and my thoughts returned to the predicament at hand. The pieces didn't add up.

How did they find me? I had been extremely careful, telling no-one where I was staying — not even the person I had trusted — Janet. She had too big a stake in winning the case to see any harm come to me. "She needed my expertise," I told myself.

We had been extremely careful in our conversations, using burner phones and different numbers for every call. I was also extra diligent in using my computer, disconnecting Wi-Fi capabilities at the cabin. It was technology though, and I guess nothing is foolproof. Still, it seemed the probability of them finding me through electronic tracking was very low.

As for being followed on my various forays away from the cabin, I was certain no-one had followed me. The back roads leading to the cabin were all one lane, and I made sure to pull off the side of the road at regular intervals to see if someone was tailing me — precautions I had picked up in defensive driving courses.

My father, a career foreign embassy employee who had worked in some very dangerous places, had enrolled me in them. Even though my job had, up until now, been quite vanilla, he had insisted, saying, "Renee, you can never be too careful. You never know what life will throw at you, so you had best be prepared." I silently thanked him, wishing for all the world that he was still alive — the same wish I had for my mother. He was still with me in spirit though, and his lessons in survival had served me well.

I hadn't checked for tracking devices on the Porsche. Janet suggested someone may have placed something on the vehicle during my misadventure at the resort, but it was certainly too late now to check now, as that amazing piece of automotive genius was now likely just a burned-out husk. I don't believe they tracked me on the Porsche anyway, since they couldn't identify my vehicle. There were cameras at the resort, for sure, but some outside criminal organization surely wouldn't have access to them.

Something was tickling the back of my brain, just enough to tell me I was missing something important, but not loud enough to give me the answer.

My mind grew weary from these thoughts, and I laid back, the warmth of the fire pulling me toward sleep. This is when an idea came to me. Listening to my gut, which was usually the right thing to do, I decided to call Dan. I trusted him, and knew that although he worked in the same firm as Janet, they were in separate office buildings. With the trial approaching, I needed some answers from a trusted, independent source. *I will call him tomorrow*, I thought to myself.

As dawn broke, my eyes fluttered open as my mind struggled to make sense of where I was — and what I was doing there. The horrors of the previous day then came flooding back. I closed my eyes in a vain attempt to erase those memories, and when they re-opened, I was treated to a sight that washed away my anxiety. It was a doe, full of grace, with her fawn following closely on spindly legs, ambling along in my direction. I was lying perfectly still, and must have been downwind, as they didn't seem to notice me. This beautiful moment had brought me back to the present, and as only nature has a way of doing, settled me.

When they had traveled on their way, I ate a tin of anchovies, paired with parmesan flavored crackers, washing it down with a coke that had graced the picnic basket. *Not exactly a breakfast of champions*, I thought while wiping my sleeve across my mouth. Sometimes it just is what it is. The smell of woodsmoke had permeated my clothing, which I noticed while shaking off loose blades of grass and pine needles. I took another swig of coke and climbed into the Bentley, feeling like a trespasser in this fine luxury automobile.

I had a plan — one based more on a lack of options than anything. I would return to the cabin, see where things stood, and then go from there. Backtracking would be challenging, but I could follow tracks on the old, unused logging roads and the rushing river…

A memory flashed through my brain, intruding on my thoughts. The river — Laura had once mentioned in passing that she and Tony had what she called a secluded "getaway cabin" downriver from the main house. She was a budding novelist and told me she would go there to write.

With this memory, my plan took a new direction. I will return to the main cabin, grab some clothes and provisions, and search for the getaway cabin. I don't know exactly where it is, but it should be easy to search for. The best part is that no one knows about it. It will be a safe place to hole up for the next two days before the trial starts.

Driving slowly, I followed landmarks memorized from the day before, car tracks in the few places they were visible, and made my way back toward the cabin. When I was close to a mile away, I drove the Bentley into the woods, where I found a good hiding place in a thick stand of Juniper. I would go the rest of the way on foot.

The walk through the woods was pleasant, and I found it to be quite enjoyable. That was, until I drew nearer, and picked up the acrid scent of burned fuel and the ruined contents of the garage. I crept forward keeping to the thickest foliage until I neared the back side of the garage.

Parked about 20 feet away, under cover, and thankfully out of range of the flames, sat the Harley. I recalled that I left it parked there when I returned from my near-death adventure to pick up the case materials. I had been understandably edgy and wanted to have it within easy reach in case I needed to run. I silently thanked myself for my foresight, knowing I had saved it from the flames. For now, given the circumstances, it would be my "go to" method of transportation, able to cover ground that the Bentley couldn't. There was no rain in the forecast, which made it the perfect choice for me.

I left the Harley, and the safety of the woods, and worked my way around the back side of the barn, passing a few places where the interior of the hidden garage was exposed. Glancing briefly inside, I had to turn away. I know that cars and motorcycles are not sentient beings, but my fondness for them was real, and to me, it was as if the world had just lost some very special inhabitants.

I peered around the corner of the barn and breathed a sigh of relief. The cabin was still standing. They hadn't returned to torch it. In fact, given that nature seemed to be unbothered, and the sounds of chirping and rustling in the leaves, it appeared that they hadn't returned at all. They may have believed me dead, and planned to come back to verify once the garage was cool enough to enter.

I decided to move fast, so I bolted toward the cabin, entered my key in the side door and hurried inside. The creepy feeling I had experienced the night before came rushing back, but this time while I was *inside* the house. The hairs were standing on the back of my neck, and it took all my willpower to stay the course and take care of business. I had some important packing to do.

I found a tote bag and gathered some provisions, not knowing whether or how well the getaway cabin was stocked. I then grabbed my dress clothes for trial, along with a change of casual clothes and some toiletries. I wanted more than anything to get the heck out of here, but I had one more thing to get. I found the dresser and opened the top drawer, grabbing the key to the Harley.

It was time to leave.

I ran awkwardly from the house and across the yard, carrying my load. When I reached the Harley, I stuffed the contents from the totes into the carry compartments and brought the bike to life.

On a whim, or perhaps some subconscious survival instinct, I turned the key and silenced the bike. I had an idea. Stepping back to the storage compartments, I ran my hand under them and onto the smooth metal of the bike. Reaching further underneath, my fingers grazed something that felt out of place — a protrusion of some sort. I removed the storage compartment from its holder and immediately spotted it — a small round transmitting device.

My heart raced as my mind struggled to comprehend the implications. After a thorough search of all the nooks and crannies, as well as the inside of the compartments, I came away satisfied that there was only one bug. I considered smashing it against a rock, an act that would quell the anger that this violation of my privacy had created, but thought better of it. Instead, I carefully concealed the bug in an old jar of nails on the top shelf. *That should do it*, I thought to myself.

It was time to ride.

Donning my helmet, I shot off through an opening in the trees and onto the logging trail in the direction of the Bentley. The trip back to the SUV took no time at all, and I had soon returned to my second lifeline. My only remaining modes of transportation were the Harley and the Bentley, since I had left a path of destruction and danger in my wake, one that consumed the other vehicles. Having found the bug on the Harley, I conducted a thorough search of the Bentley, looking in the wheel wells, and even climbing beneath the vehicle, shining my flashlight over every square inch.

To my great relief, it was clean of tracking devices.

I pulled a bag containing my electronics and computer from the Bentley, and slung it over my shoulder and across my body. Then I set off toward the river on the Harley. I knew the general direction of the river and zigzagged across logging roads and down game trails until I reached the riverbank. There was a trail, or what might best be described as a narrow, overgrown, barely passable path, leading along the riverbank.

"Should I go right or left?" I asked myself. The decision was made for me when I looked to my left and saw where the muddy earth was dotted with cattails, indicating swampy terrain. It was impassable on the bike. I would go right and, if worse came to worse, I would circle back and head further down river until I found a decent path to explore.

As it turned out, going right was the correct decision. Not far upstream was a bend in the river, where about fifty yards in, on a grassy knoll surrounded by a stand of Douglas fir trees — the Christmas tree variety — stood the cabin. The dwelling was crafted to fit naturally into the surrounding environment. So much so, in fact, that it was nearly invisible from the riverbank. I never would have found it if I hadn't been looking for it.

I rode slowly up, parking the bike out of sight, and walked to the door with my few earthly possessions. Inserting my only key, the same one that opened the doors to the main cabin, I held my breath — saying a silent prayer that it would turn the lock.

CHAPTER 22

A reassuring turn of the key ended my concern.

Stepping into the cabin, I was instantly amazed. *Some "getaway cabin"*, I thought to myself. *I could live here the rest of my life and be perfectly happy.* The heart pine floor, mahogany paneled walls, and soft leather couches and chairs that formed a semi-circle around the stone hearth fireplace gave the place an intimate, cozy feel.

And it was indeed a great place to write, with a large walnut desk, complete with the most modern computer equipment, set before a large picture window overlooking the river. A small but efficient kitchen held a fully stocked freezer and fridge with a few essentials. There was even a small wine cooler set beneath the cabinet drawers.

Along a far wall was posted a map of the surrounding forest, with trails and old logging roads noted by dotted and straight lines. Laura had continued to be my saving grace, and I silently thanked her again. I memorized the map, and turned back to my tasks. There was a lot to do and little time to do it.

I set my laptop on the desk and went out to retrieve my belongings from the bike. The brief journey brought me back to the cabin, my boots thudding across the wooden floor and into a back bedroom, where I hung my badly wrinkled business suit in the closet, and laid my other clothing items on the bed. With that task accomplished, I headed back to the main room and set the case materials on a chair beside the desk.

I desperately needed a shower, but first, I would call Dan. The burner phone in my hand reminded me that it was my last; a problem, but not an insurmountable one. I decided it was best to put some distance between me and the cabin for the call. I don't want anyone to find me, and not just for my sake. I can't stomach any more responsibility for the damage to Laura and Tony's properties. As it stands, I don't know how I will ever make it up to them.

My selfish motive was to enjoy a ride through the backwoods on the Harley — a real blast.

After leaving the cabin and locking the door behind me, I headed down the game trail along the river until I reached the point I had entered earlier, and made my way inland down overgrown logging roads, following the map by memory. Once satisfied that I was far enough away from the cabin, I made the call.

Dan answered on the third ring, from a cell phone number I had used to contact him before. I dared not call the main office since they would ask for my name, and secrecy was my most precious commodity. "Hello Dan, this is Renee," I said, skipping formalities.

"It is great to hear from you doctor Strick— I mean, Renee. I've heard bits and pieces about the events surrounding the Covington case and knew that you were in some danger. I'm glad to know that you are alright. I must apologize as well. We are a very large firm and somewhat compartmentalized, so I've been out of the loop on Jill's case since Logan's case had settled. Would you be willing to fill me in?"

"Sure," I said, relieved to finally be able to tell someone the whole story. I couldn't be one-hundred percent certain that Dan was trustworthy, but there was no-one else in the firm for whom to turn. The jury was out on Janet, given all that had transpired. I had to trust my instincts, take a deep breath, and step out on faith.

I told him the whole story, from beginning to end, only omitting my present and former locations, and details about the vehicles I had borrowed.

After I gave him a few minutes to soak it all in, I finally asked, "So, what are your thoughts?"

I could hear him breathe a deep sigh through the phone, and then he responded. "First, Renee, let me say how sorry I am to hear all of this. You should never be put in such grave danger over a case where you are testifying as an expert. I don't know Janet all that well, having only been with the firm a little over a year and, as I mentioned, the firm is quite large and compartmentalized. To be honest, few of the attorneys here socialize regularly, and we often know very little about one another. My advice for you would be to trust no-one, and keep your location completely secret."

Dan hesitated for a moment. "Wait, hold on a sec. I'm bringing up the trial calendar. It looks like you are scheduled to testify this coming Monday. You should arrive at the courthouse, room 206B, at nine a.m. You will be one of the first to testify."

This should have been a conversation with Janet — learning the details of the trial schedule — but I didn't feel comfortable calling her given all that had happened, and not knowing whether she was connected somehow, even if innocently, to how that murderous bunch had found me.

"That is very helpful, Dan," I replied with complete sincerity. "Please let Janet know I'm aware of the trial date and will come prepared. Please also tell her that, given all that has happened, I'm going underground until the trial for my own safety. I'm sure she'll understand."

I paused, as a thought came to me. "And Dan, would you please let her know that I'll meet with the authorities — namely, the FBI — once things play out a bit more."

"No problem," said Dan. "I didn't know that the FBI wanted to meet with you. I'm friends with a few of the agents who I play basketball with on weekends, and no-one ever mentioned anything to me."

"That's interesting. Janet said that your firm would be handling all the arrangements and the authorities would be working through her office to arrange meetings and interviews with me."

"That doesn't make sense," said Dan, sounding perplexed. "The FBI doesn't work *through* our firm, or any attorneys in it. They might ask for help in finding you, but we don't facilitate meetings on behalf of the FBI."

With Dan's words, suspicion now had a firm grip on me. He was right, of course. How could I have been so stupid to take what Janet told me at face value?

"Listen, Renee, we need to be super careful. Something very fishy is going on. I'll make some quiet inquiries, but you need to continue to stay completely off the grid until trial. As for Monday, I don't know, and don't want to know how you will be arriving, but let's plan to meet at the back entrance to the courthouse at eight-thirty a.m. sharp, and I will escort you into the building. I know a secret entrance."

"Thank you," I replied, fighting back emotions that had been welling up inside me. I could feel an emotional dam beginning to burst, so I finished the call by saying, "You have no idea how much I appreciate this, Dan."

I smashed the sim card on a rock and threw the phone deep into the brush. Then, I sat alone in the silence of the forest and cried. I had to go this alone. I couldn't endanger my friends and colleagues, or my brother's family who lived in California. It was a great comfort, however, to know that Dan would support me.

There was little time to feel sorry for myself though, so I wiped my eyes with the tail of my shirt, and hopped back on the Harley.

Riding through the woods, and experiencing the freedom of movement, I returned to the getaway cabin all too soon. I have a few days to prepare my testimony but will reserve the remainder of this one enjoying the safety and solitude of the cabin, along with a good meal and fine wine from Laura and Tony's collection. I will also enjoy a much needed, and anticipated, lengthy hot shower.

Later, feeling refreshed from the shower and sated from a hot meal and glass of Silver Oak Cabernet, I built a fire and sat back in one of the large, comfortable leather chairs to take stock of my situation.

I just couldn't shake the feeling that there was more to what I had experienced than met the eye.

Could Janet be involved somehow? It was beyond imagining that the attorney representing Jill and the Covingtons would be working for the criminal enterprise that had her abducted and intended to traffic her.

So much didn't add up. Take the FBI, for instance.

It was strange that the FBI, investigating a criminal enterprise involved in human trafficking, hadn't gone to great lengths to speak with me. I had been abducted, after all, and had information that would be helpful to them. And Dan made a great point. It didn't make sense that they would be working only through the law firm, and not moving heaven and earth to speak with me directly. Had Janet been forthcoming with them? Was she being honest with me?

Things weren't adding up, and I now felt strongly about one thing — I didn't trust Janet.

I will do my part at the trial, providing my opinion on safety and security measures that are the responsibility of the hotel operator, but will keep any thoughts about the culpability of a criminal enterprise working behind the scenes to myself.

Dead tired, and knowing that I needed to be on my game, I slept in the next morning and went for a long walk along the riverbank.

I was reminded, during my walk, of a story my university mentor used to tell. It was about a young boy who was vacationing with his family at a state park, staying at a cabin along a river much like this one. The boy, only eight years old, had wandered down a trail — without his parent's knowledge or permission — along the stream on his way, it was told, to the park lodge. There was a large jar of candy at the reception desk and he wanted some chocolate drops that his parents had told him he couldn't have.

Somewhere along the way, he had stepped into the river. For what reason, no-one would ever know. He had slipped or been pulled by the current and carried downstream — to be found two days later by a hiker. His parents, distraught, and seeking compensation for an injustice they believed needed a remedy, sued the park, claiming that there should have been barriers, or at least warning signs at access points along the river.

The park countered with the argument that they were protected by statute — specifically, one called a Recreation User Statute. This state law protected landowners and land managing agencies such as state parks from liability where someone was injured or killed while engaging in a recreational activity on the land. Attorneys for the state argued that the boy was engaged in a recreational activity, therefore invoking the protections from liability afforded by the statute.

Attorneys for the boy's parents countered with the argument that it was not certain whether the boy was engaged in a recreational activity when he entered the water — things like skipping stones or hunting for crawfish — but could just have easily slipped in while making his way to the lodge, while engaging in what they defined as "transportation," and not recreation, removing the park from statutory protections.

Other arguments for the plaintiff were that warning signage would have prevented the tragedy, and that the area where he entered the water was known to drop off sharply in depth, creating a hazard that could not be seen from shore — a hidden danger.

The defense countered with arguments that even had there been a sign, an eight-year-old boy could not have understood its significance, and that erecting barriers along every access point in the river that posed some element of danger would be cost-prohibitive, and ruin the natural beauty of the park. The defense attorneys also deflected the blame to the parents, those responsible for their son.

In the end, the court held that there was a heightened risk of danger at the access point where the child was believed to have entered the river, and therefore it was the duty of the park to have erected a sign warning of the drop-off and danger of drowning. The court apportioned 40 percent of the fault to the parents for failing to supervise their child, and 60 percent of the fault to the park for failing to provide a warning sign. Since the parents had sued for one million dollars, this meant that the park was liable for 60 percent of monetary damages, or $600,000. It was a good lesson in the importance of providing warning signs, even where their effectiveness might be unknown.

After the walk, I returned to the cabin and reviewed my notes and case materials. I also treated myself to some of the provisions Laura and Tony had left at the cabin. Soon, I would need to do some shopping of my own.

Before I knew it, my final days of safety and solitude had passed, and the day of the trial was upon me.

CHAPTER 23

I woke at 5 a.m., unable to fall back into the safe and comforting land of dreams, and began mental preparations for the big day. I was giving testimony at trial, but not just any trial, one that would quite possibly alter the course of my life, and others. The outcomes were unknown, and some were quite frightening, so I did what I always did in challenging and complex situations with uncertain outcomes — I compartmentalized and focused on the small pieces that made up the whole.

The first order of business was to prepare both mentally and physically, so I pulled out my yoga mat and worked through my routine, breathing deeply, and building a meditative state. The cabin was dark and quiet, making it easy to push out intrusive and anxiety-producing thoughts, and achieve a fair level of inner peace.

An hour later, I rose, rolled up my mat and, feeling physically and mentally re-charged, brewed a pot of green tea. When it brewed to my liking, I added sourwood honey and milk, and sat at the desk looking out across the river. The sun illuminated the crests of countless whitecaps as the sparkling liquid journeyed downstream. It was at once mesmerizing and beautiful.

After finishing the cup of tea, I walked to the sink and set it inside. I pulled a thawed bagel from the fridge and popped it in the toaster, then poured a glass of milk and enjoyed a simple breakfast. It helped me not to have a full stomach.

The shower that followed was quick and served the dual purpose of cleaning off the grime and steaming my business suit — the one I hung ever so carefully on the edge of the shower so the vapor would draw out the wrinkles.

Once dry, I dressed in the set of casual clothes hastily gathered from the main cabin, and carefully folded my suit on the bed. I then threw on a black leather jacket from a rack of expensive coats in Laura's closet, and carried the suit, accessories, and a pair of dress shoes, along with the case files, to the Harley and loaded all of it into the carry compartments. Timing my meeting with Dan for 8:30, I calculated the time it would take to arrive at the courthouse and park.

I had fifteen minutes of time to fill, so I walked down to the river to ease the burning sensation of anxiety in my gut. It worked — at least some — as I fought to keep negative and anxious thoughts from my mind. I need to stay calm and positive — not just for me, but also for Jill. Thoughts of Jill, that brave young woman, anchored me, and my anxiety turned to resolve.

With my fifteen minutes up, I strapped on my helmet, hopped on the Harley, and headed off to meet my fate.

I had mapped out a way to reach a section of county road far away from anyone who might be lying in wait for me as I headed toward town. It required zigzagging down old logging roads, traversing a game trail or two, and traveling across a field, but the result was as intended. I hit the county road far north of where anyone might expect me to be and entered town from a direction that would seem impossible to anyone trying to anticipate my moves.

When I reached town, I parked my bike a few blocks away from the courthouse. I placed my belongings in a backpack and, keeping the helmet in place to hide my identity, made my way to the back entrance of the courthouse. I was right on time.

Dan was waiting for me there as promised, and escorted me into the building through an unmarked door that, I learned, on rare occasions was used to move high profile people in and out of the building. He then led me quickly down a dimly lit corridor, and finally up a set of stairs leading to a waiting room intended for attorneys preparing for trial.

"You can use this room to change," said Dan with a deadpan look. "Unless you would prefer the more "biker casual" look."

The gleam dancing in his eyes at this poor attempt at humor made me smile and brought with it the stark realization that I really liked this man.

"Oh, I think I'll upgrade a bit," I said. "I wouldn't want to be outclassed by some cheesy, low-life attorney."

"Good idea," replied Dan with a wide grin spread across his face. "No sense in letting this 'cheesy, low-life lawyer' upstage you. Just come on out when you're ready. I'll wait for you in the conference room down the hall."

Five minutes later, I was outside the conference room, dressed and ready for battle.

"Let's go," said Dan, now fully serious. "Janet has agreed to let me sit in on the case as an observer. Playing on her ego, I told her she was well respected as a litigator, and I wanted to learn from seeing her perform at trial. She actually *blushed* when I told her that."

"I'm glad you'll be there," I said, noticing that *he* was blushing now.

After two previous days of procedural maneuvering, the attorneys were ready for their opening arguments. This, I knew, could take up most of the morning. Janet, as the lead plaintiff's attorney, went first. A critical piece of her case was to persuade the jury that the resort, and its upper management, were at fault for the actions perpetrated by the manager, Johnny Grubbs.

Janet began her opening statement, standing directly in front of the jury box in a non-threatening posture, thanking them for their service, and fulfilling their civic duty. She then launched into the legal claims that comprised the foundation of the plaintiff's case — false imprisonment, assault and battery, infliction of emotional distress, and negligence — telling the jury that they would see indisputable proof that the manager and his employer were guilty of all these wrongs against Jill and her family.

Janet spent the next 20 minutes talking about the involvement and culpability of the manager, but oddly, only drawing a thin line of culpability to the upper resort management. She did mention, however, on several occasions a connection to a mysterious criminal enterprise that was ostensibly involved in human trafficking, and how it was believed they were long gone now. She said firmly that the resort was now completely safe.

I almost rose from my seat. Long gone? Completely safe? I thought, with bile rising in my throat. I was, myself, abducted, duct taped and bound, barely a week ago. What the hell is she talking about!?

Dan sensed my anguish and turned to look back at me. He silently mouthed, "Stay calm."

He was right, and I settled back into my seat, my mind now roused and hyperactive. My thoughts drifted back to the Harley as Janet droned on in the background.

The bug, my mind questioned. *Was it the reason my hiding place had been discovered?* That would depend on when it was placed there, I reasoned. If Shrek and his gang had placed it there when they torched the garage and attempted to torch me with it, then it wasn't the reason they had found me.

If, however, it had been attached to the bike earlier, then it could have been the reason they found me. *But when could it have been placed on my bike, if not while at the cabin?* The only possible time was when I rode into town to pick up the case materials from Janet's paralegal, Harvey. He helped transfer the case materials to the compartments, and could have placed it there while I was distracted. No-one else was near the bike or had the opportunity, so by process of elimination, if it had been placed prior to the attack on the cabin, it had to have been him. That would mean…

Dear God, it can't be. If that's the case, it would mean Janet is complicit. Was she working for, or threatened or paid off by, whatever criminal enterprise was involved? It seemed she was sandbagging her opening statement, not working very hard at all to draw in whatever evil enterprise Grubbs had been serving. Or was all this a product of an overactive imagination, with my paranoia running amok? Perhaps my original theory was correct, and the bad guys had found my location by tracing my calls to Janet, and they had been the ones to place the tracking device on the Harley in case I survived the fire.

My mind was whirring with the possibilities, and I was finding it extremely difficult to focus on the task at hand — providing my testimony in the case. I took deep breaths, my experience with meditation allowing me to enter a more relaxed state, and listened to the opening statement of the defense.

With the door now firmly open, the attorney for the defense spent thirty minutes working to convince the jury that, while the manager, Grubbs, was clearly at fault, he was acting on behalf of an unknown third party with criminal intent. He added that, as the plaintiff's attorney made clear, the criminal enterprise behind it all was long gone, rendering the resort a completely safe place to visit.

The way the case was heading, I reasoned, Jill and her family would only receive damages for which the manager was liable. This would amount to practically nothing. And worse, the resort and its upper management, those ultimately responsible for what would surely be a lifetime of emotional trauma for Jill, would get off scot-free.

My stomach churned at the thought.

When opening statements had concluded, and for reasons only known to the judge and attorneys in the case, the judge called a recess and said that the court would re-adjourn in thirty minutes.

Janet made eye contact and headed my way. "Hello Dr. Strickland," she said in a honeyed voice, "Please follow me to the conference room. We have something to discuss."

I looked over at Dan, who briefly nodded, and blindly followed Janet into whatever storm might follow.

CHAPTER 24

Once seated at the conference table, Janet opened a folder and looked at me intently. Less human, and more snake-like, her gaze was that of a viper, sensing the million delicate, imperceptible vibrations emitted from a potential adversary — or prey — that signals whether to strike.

"I am so glad that you are here to testify," said Janet, in a cold and implacable tone. "If you will, let's go over your testimony to ensure that we are on the same page. We would normally have done this earlier, and I apologize, but circumstances have made that impossible."

Circumstances, I thought bitterly. My near-death experiences were more than "circumstances."

"You should also know before we start that the defense has made us an offer. It is not what we wanted, but they have agreed to a settlement amount that might be considered reasonable. My co-counsel and I are considering it, but I would like for the jury to hear your testimony first, in the event that it shakes more money loose from them. We are, after all, seeking *justice* here, and want what is best for Jill and her family."

"I understand," I said, unconvinced that Janet wanted anything for anyone other than herself.

"Well, let's get to it then. The defense has not named you as a witness and, as you know, can only cross-examine you on the subject matter of the direct examination. I plan to restrict your testimony to the negligence claim against the manager and resort, to whatever extent they may be negligent."

"If I may ask," I said, my curiosity too strong to contain, "will it be important for me to address whatever criminal element is behind Jill's abduction, and should I mention my own incident on the top floor?"

"Let's stay away from those issues, not only for your own safety and wellbeing but also for that of Jill. I'm afraid that going too far down that road will not end well."

"Are you concerned for my safety, or is it something else?" I blurted out.

As soon as the words left my lips, I knew it was a mistake.

Janet's eyes turned cold and hard. *"Of course,* it is for your safety. What other motive could there possibly be?"

Her words were so hard and cruel, it left me stunned. I said, stammering slightly, "I don't know, it just seemed from your opening statement that you were soft on the resort management. I thought that was where the deep pockets were, and the best chance for Jill to receive *justice.*"

Janet didn't respond right away. Instead, she studied me intently. When she did respond, it was all business. "Dr. Strickland, with all due respect, we hired you to give your expert opinion on certain matters in this case. It would be best if we focused on *your* testimony."

I could see that the matter would not be discussed further, and simply nodded my agreement.

"I will begin the direct examination with open-ended questions about your educational background and experience that supports your expertise in sport, hospitality and recreation safety."

"I am prepared for that," I said confidently.

"Once we have discussed your background — and I'll fill in any blanks you might have missed to bolster your credibility — we will move on to your opinion. I would like to focus your opinion on the standard of care for cameras in elevators and hallways, and the public nature of hallways, even on the top floor. I will also ask your opinion of the safety measures associated with the number and location of security personnel, or other security measures that a hotel should have in place to prevent the *incident* at issue."

"OK," I said, "but I'll have to be honest. The court needs to know that I was also abducted — long after Jill had been abducted — and the same thing happened to me. The resort took no action to fix the safety issues that led to Jill's abduction. That *has* to matter. Otherwise, all you have is my testimony that cameras in the hallways are the industry standard, which will surely be refuted by their expert."

Janet slammed her fist on the table with enough force to rattle a set of pens resting on the surface. "I'll do the lawyering. But if you must know, putting in cameras after the incident would be considered a subsequent remedial measure, and not allowed as evidence."

"But under the federal rules," I countered, "this might be allowable since it could prove that it would have been possible to prevent the abduction with safer conditions. Cameras have been shown to provide a deterrent to criminal acts. It would probably have prevented my abduction as well."

"Enough!" yelled Janet, further revealing a temper I had not seen before. "Will you testify or not as to what is within the boundaries of your testimony that I am setting? If not, we will seek a refund for your services and take appropriate legal action."

With downcast eyes, and appearing submissive, I replied, "OK, I will play by your rules."

"Good. Let's get this over with then, shall we?"

The walk back to the courtroom was tense, with neither of us saying a word.

When I took the witness stand, I saw them — several of the goons I had seen attack the house and burn the garage. Oddly, instead of fear, I experienced a feeling of extreme calm.

I had made my decision.

Janet walked with confidence to the witness stand, where I had moments before been sworn in. She began, as promised, with an open-ended question about my background and experience. I responded in clear and concise sentences, telling everyone within earshot what I had done to deserve to sit in this chair as an expert in the case.

Satisfied that my credibility had been sufficiently established, Janet moved on to my opinions in the matter. I stated my opinions succinctly, providing only the essential information — that which would inform the court on the matter of the standard of care for hotels and resorts in providing for the safety and security of their guests.

Janet, appearing pleased with my testimony, said, "I have no more—"

"Aren't you going to ask me about the time that *I* was abducted at this *same resort* on the *very same floor* as this brave young woman, Jill? And why did you have a tracker put on my bike by your paralegal Harvey — one that led those goons sitting in the second row to my location, intent on ending my life? I, like everyone else in this courtroom, want to know who is behind all of this. And are you crooked as well?"

My body shook at the realization of what I had just said. It was as if my words had come from the mouth of someone else.

There was a three second moment of silence, and then you would have thought that I had just tossed a bucket of live snakes in the courtroom. Janet turned pale, then yelled, "Objection!" and stuttered, "I have ended my questioning. My witness cannot interject her own comments."

Simultaneously, the attorneys on both sides stood, as well as the thugs on the second row. I could hear murmurs and gasps across the courtroom, with the commotion steadily increasing. I heard, as if at a distance, the judge's gavel slam hard on the bench — once, twice, and then a third time — as she yelled "Order in the court!"

As if this were all happening to someone else, like in a movie, I saw Dan leap over the aisle and into a row near the front — with people pushed aside and falling. And then… I heard two gunshots — and saw Dan driving into the two thugs like a linebacker making the big play. This was followed by drawn guns and serious, official looking men and women storming the courtroom.

All hell was breaking loose.

I would later learn that a bullet had lodged in the front panel of the witness stand — mere inches from causing me serious injury or death.

I was released from my stupor when Dan approached me, followed by a man and woman who flashed their FBI badges. "Follow us," they said with urgency, leading me quickly out of the courtroom, down the back halls that I had traversed earlier, and out the back door to a waiting black SUV — the standard FBI vehicle.

To my surprise and delight, Dan slid into the seat beside me. "You sure know how to cause a stir, Dr. Strickland." We both laughed until we cried, releasing a tsunami of emotion.

CHAPTER 25

I spent the remainder of the day with the FBI. They treated me with respect and professionalism, as I recounted all that happened since agreeing to take this case as an expert witness. I left no detail unspoken, except for the existence and location of the getaway cabin. I needed to keep something for myself, and besides, it wasn't relevant to their investigation.

As they were wrapping up, I asked the lead agent, a weathered veteran of the agency, if they had any idea who was behind the abductions of Jill and I, and the sex trafficking ring. He looked at me with knowing eyes, hearing the desperation in my voice, and decided to throw me a hint.

"Well, he said, in a thick southern drawl, I can't tell you much since this is an ongoing investigation, but I will say that it isn't some unknown criminal enterprise lurking in the shadows." He winked, and then said, "We think it is closer to home."

With that breadcrumb, he ended the interview, and we said our goodbyes. He said that he would be in touch if the agency needed anything else from me and added that I should lie low for a few days until things got ironed out. He even offered FBI protection and a stay at a local safehouse.

I respectfully declined, wishing to get back to the safety and seclusion of the cabin.

A moment after he left the room, leaving me alone with my thoughts and unanswered questions, Dan entered and escorted me out.

"So, what do you plan to do now?" he asked.

"The FBI offered protection and a stay at their safehouse, but I declined. I would rather head back to a place I know tucked way back in the woods."

"I can understand that," said Dan. "I would probably choose the same if I were in your shoes. I imagine you need some time alone."

"I do," I said. "It probably won't need to be a long stay though, as the special agent in charge told me that I should 'lie low for a *few* days.' They must be closing in on the perpetrators. He also hinted that a shadowy criminal enterprise wasn't behind all of this — that it was closer to home."

"Hmm. I wonder…"

"You wonder what?" I asked, already suspecting the answer.

"I wonder if someone or some group within the upper management of the resort was responsible? I learned from speaking with several agents while you were being interviewed that the thugs in the courtroom were hired, and not direct employees of a criminal enterprise. They were basically thugs for hire — independent contractors."

"That was my suspicion," I said. Someone wanted me to think that there was a mysterious criminal enterprise behind all of this, to create misdirection. What we now suspect would point to an inside job — the resort itself being responsible for the abductions. This would also explain why Janet sandbagged her opening statement, and was so soft on the resort when arguing her case. She was probably paid well to lessen or eliminate the blame on the resort. She may have even been playing both sides against the middle, taking her percentage of a settlement if it was more than the resort was paying her under the table."

"A very clever scheme," said Dan. "I've never seen it done before. I guess there is a first time for everything. It will be interesting to see what the FBI finds. Janet is quite cagey, and has not said much, instead opting to lawyer-up. I believe it stands to reason, however, that she directed the placement of the bug on your bike."

"I'm sure of it," I said.

Dan paused; his brow wrinkled in thought. "Do you remember telling me about the video taken by the pool. I believe you said that you saw a wealthy-looking man wearing sunglasses and a gold chain sitting by the pool. Do you still have that video?

"It's with my files, but I do have a screenshot of him that I saved to Google docs. I might be able to bring it up on your phone using my password."

A minute or two later, I accessed the photo and downloaded it to his phone.

Dan looked at the picture intently and said, "This guy looks very familiar. I'll share the photo with the FBI. He might come up in one of their criminal databases — and might just be the key to everything. I bet that when you shared your suspicions with Janet, it set events in motion that led to their attempt to silence you. They probably believed that you were getting too close to the truth.

"You mean *kill* me." I said, my voice tinged with anger.

"OK, I won't soft pedal you. That is a more direct and accurate way to put it. The good news, though, is that once this is all sorted out, I'm sure there will be someone you can sue."

"Spoken like a true lawyer," I joked.

Dan shrugged. "Well, you *have* suffered greatly."

I *loved* lawyers and was feeling an inkling of that emotion toward this one in particular.

Dan walked me to my bike, making a quick stop along the way to help me pick up some fresh provisions. The carrying compartments were now empty — having given my case materials to the authorities — so I filled them up with goodies from the market. I also checked the bike carefully for tracking devices. You can never be too careful.

I shared a warm hug with this great guy, and sped off on the Harley, heading toward the open road.

Heading the bike toward the west, with the intent to swing well out of town and circle back north of my destination, I hit an open stretch of highway — and let my guard down.

It was a mistake.

The bullet from the marksman in the truck behind me struck my back tire, the sound of flapping and grinding loud enough to be heard over the rushing wind. An experienced biker, I knew not to make sudden movements, but to keep riding in a straight line, and ease into using the front brake, slowing the bike gradually.

I risked a peek over my shoulder and saw the truck bearing down on me. It looked like one of the pickups from my near escape back in town, after picking up the case materials —

what now seemed like a lifetime ago. I guess these boys hadn't got the message that the gig was up.

The *ping, ping* of bullets glancing off the bike's frame made it clear they hadn't.

The gunfire stopped when I had finally coasted the bike to the shoulder. I could hear cars passing by now — potential witnesses — and guessed the thugs didn't want to risk being seen engaged in an act of murder. Change of plans for the driver, I guessed, as he hadn't tried to crash into me. Instead, he idled up behind me, looking like the good Samaritan helping a disabled vehicle, as the cars passed.

The tires had barely stopped rolling when the doors opened and four men jumped out, all poorly concealing an array of weapons.

Not wanting to stop and chat, I dove off my bike and headlong down a steep embankment, my unimpeded roll cushioned by the tall Rye grass growing along the slope. I was unaware of the bullets whizzing by as I crashed headfirst into the unknown.

My journey down the hill ended as my shoulder and helmet collided with a large boulder, sending me cartwheeling over the top and landing flat in the grass beyond. Taking stock of my injuries, I noticed my shoulder ached, and I was slightly dazed, but otherwise everything was OK. The helmet had clearly saved my life.

Crawling behind the boulder, and feeling the cold comfort of its protection, I risked a look above, only to have my worst fears realized. The murderous band of men from the truck were carefully working their way down the embankment toward my position. Taking no chances, and eager to earn the distinction of being the first to put a bullet in me, they advanced upon my position with weapons drawn.

I have clearly ticked somebody off.

Out of options, I ducked behind the boulder and waited for the inevitable. I could hear malicious laughter as they questioned whether to have their way with me before they put a bullet in my brain. They were getting close.

My hand closed around a large rock, ready to make a last stand and inflict some damage before I died.

Just as all hope was lost, the sound of a loud, commanding voice rang out from atop the embankment — telling my pursuers to drop their weapons. My pursuers clearly didn't comply, even though they were in a poor strategic position for a gunfight, as the next sound I heard was gunfire — and lots of it.

I lay flat behind the boulder, holding my breath and hoping — like in a film — that the good guys would prevail. The grunts from the men near me, and the gradual decrease in the sound of gunfire — culminating in a few *pop pops* and then silence — left me feeling hopeful. Still, I dared not move from my position.

Looking up, a few moments later, I saw my savior. It was Dan — again coming to my rescue, this time with a group of armed FBI agents.

"My gosh, girl," he said. "Does trouble never stop looking for you?"

"It looks that way," I replied with a smirk, pulling off my helmet and letting my thick, ebony hair fall freely to my shoulders. "I think my nine lives are up though."

Gazing directly into his dazzling blue eyes, I smiled and said, "I'm also beginning to realize that I have a guardian angel. How in the world did you and the cavalry find me, and just in the nick of time?"

"OK," said Dan. "I have a confession to make. Seeing as the danger surrounding you has not yet been snuffed out, I provided you with a secret escort to ensure no-one was following you, at least until you were near your hideout. Given that I'm just a lawyer, and not a trained FBI field agent, I thought it wise to bring along some reinforcements."

"I would normally be mad about the attention, since I can usually take care of myself, but under the circumstances, I'm very thankful."

"Ma'am, we would like to take you under protective custody now if you don't mind," said one of the agents.

"I appreciate the offer, but what I really want is to fix the tire, get back on my bike, and head back to my residence for a cold one."

Dan stared at me for a long moment, a look of respect glinting in his eyes — a look shared by the hard edged, military trained agents standing next to him.

"OK," said the agent. "But you *will* receive an escort to the point where you feel confident proceeding safely."

I agreed and, after repairing the tire and tending to my scrapes and bruises, two SUVs carrying the full complement of agents escorted me home. I led them to the entrance to an old logging road, where I gave them the thumbs up, and watched them drive away.

Back in the woods, I felt safe and free again. It was the perfect medicine, as I made my way across fields, down old logging roads, and up the trail, back to the safety and comfort of the cabin.

CHAPTER 26

After a hot bath and a couple of ibuprofen, I was feeling almost back to my old self. The weather had turned, and a big thunderstorm was booming outside. Flashes of lightning flickered across the sky, and I thanked the fates that I was inside — dry and safe.

With nowhere to go, and time on my hands, I made the decision to touch up my lecture on managing risk in sport and recreational activities. As I read through my slides, I was reminded of a tragic case on which I once consulted — one involving the death of a ten-year-old boy.

As I recall, it went something like this.

A father had taken his kids to a soccer match at the local school to watch his daughter play. His two sons, aged 10 and 12, were allowed to play in a nearby area while he watched the game and cheered his daughter on. Sometime during the first period, events unfolded that would turn his world into a nightmare of epic proportions. His twelve-year-old son came running across the field, crying, and screaming, saying that his brother needed help.

The game was immediately halted, as the father, several officials, and parents raced after the boy.

He led them through a row of trees and into an open area adjacent to the field. What they found was horrifying. A portable tower, one used by the football coaches to supervise practices, lay on its side, with the ten-year-old boy lying beneath it, his neck broken.

It was later learned that he had climbed the tower, which had subsequently tipped over, throwing him to the ground and breaking his neck. He had died instantly. This had all been witnessed by his brother, who was understandably traumatized.

A few months later, the family brought a lawsuit. They sought $10 million in damages for the wrongful death of their son. It was a difficult case for the school, as one could imagine, given the loss of a child on school grounds and the negative publicity it had raised.

I was called to inspect the site the morning after the incident, while everything was still in an undisturbed state. The nature of the incident was clear, with the large metal-framed tower lying on its side, but it is what I didn't see that was most important. I didn't see any signage telling unauthorized persons to keep off the tower, nor did I see any evidence of a gate or barrier to keep people from accessing the tower.

The tower, when upright, had stood at the edge of the football practice field. From this point, about 20 yards and through a row of pine trees was the soccer field bracketed by sets of bleachers on each side of the field, one of which had been occupied by the father of the now-deceased child.

I had seen the notice of claim and mentally mapped out the way the case would play out. The plaintiffs were suing for wrongful death against the school, claiming that the school was grossly negligent — extremely careless — in having an unreasonably dangerous condition on the premises. They further claimed that it was foreseeable that a child might climb the tower, as it was also foreseeable that children would play in the area unattended while their parents watched soccer matches on the nearby field. They claimed that the tower was, in legal parlance, an "attractive nuisance" — meaning it was foreseeable that it would draw children to it, and that it was dangerous.

The defense sought to place as much blame as possible on the father — nasty business that would only add to his feelings of grief and guilt. The legal term for this was "comparative negligence" or "comparative fault" where any potential monetary damages would be proportioned among the parties according to how much fault could be attributed to each.

The defense, the side I was helping to inform through my testimony, got to the issue of whether, and to what extent, it was foreseeable a child would be in the area, and the degree of danger the tower posed.

This was admittedly a difficult case to defend, but the good thing for me was that it wasn't my job to win the case. My job was simply to render my opinion as an expert.

Thinking through the problem, I followed the protocol for managing risk that I taught my students. It consisted of two parts — severity and likelihood of injury. As for severity, the injury posed from falling from a tipped tower was potentially severe. In the present case, it was clearly severe, as it didn't get more severe than death.

As for the likelihood, or foreseeability, of injury or death, it was a bit more complicated. During the school day, when students were closely supervised and unlikely to be in the vicinity of the tower, the likelihood that a child would climb the tower was quite low.

However, it *was* likely that children, brought to the games by their parents, would wander off to play. It was also likely they would head in the direction of the football practice field to run and play, as children do, with or on whatever objects caught their interest.

Something that I stressed when teaching and conducting safety inspections was that unsupervised areas — those used for unintended purposes — were often likely to pose a threat of injury. In my opinion, the likelihood of injury from playing in the area in general, and on the tower, was moderate to high, given that the tower and support structure were found to be unstable.

Charting this out, I determined that the school had a duty to remediate, or treat, the problem. Suggested ways would include warning signage, a barrier to accessing the tower, and, of course, inspecting and repairing the tower supports. A replacement would be recommended if repairs were not feasible.

The attorney didn't like to hear it, but I really didn't see a good way to defend the case. Efforts to prevent the harm posed by the tower, in my opinion, were necessary, and would likely have prevented this tragedy. This advice, however, saved him time and trouble, and for the school officials, additional trauma, and bad publicity. It was, I concluded, best to give honest advice, a policy that I have kept to this day.

Satisfied with the edits to my lectures, I walked to the couch and lay down, my thoughts returning to the day's events. I knew I was safe at the cabin, and hoped the goons who tried to murder me today were the last of the bunch willing to take that chance.

I need more than hope though, I thought, my stubborn streak returning. *I need information.* I couldn't just sit back, with my fate decided by others. My options for communicating with the outside world, however, were limited. I couldn't call Dan, since I had used my last burner phone, and I couldn't use my laptop to send emails from here since that would be traceable. Then a thought occurred to me. *Tomorrow, I'll go back to the main cabin and use my laptop to contact Dan.* It was a risk, given the large target on my back, but one I had to take.

The next day, as planned, I set out on the Harley, my laptop secured in one of the carry compartments. Parking the bike in the woods a safe distance from the cabin, I retrieved my laptop and walked the rest of the way, mindful of any sights or sounds that would indicate danger.

When I reached the cabin, I checked the exterior for recent signs of activity, and when satisfied that I was alone, entered through the side door. Quickly setting up my laptop, I went online and opened my email, sending a brief question to Dan. It read, "Dan. I don't have much time. Have you heard anything else from the FBI?"

I waited while the clock inside my head ticked down the minutes. If they were indeed tracing signals from this cabin, I didn't have much time. *He could be at deposition, in a meeting…*

Anything is possible, I reasoned. On high alert, I sensed that time was running out. It was time to leave.

As my finger hovered over the button to log off, the reassuring "ping" of an incoming message came through. I quickly read the three short paragraphs, and copied and saved the text. My fingers flying over the keyboard, I then deleted the message, logged off and closed my computer. I sprinted out the door and locked it behind me, then ran with all my might to the edge of the forest, where several hundred yards within, sat the Harley.

Just as I entered the first row of trees, I heard the crunch of gravel as several vehicles slid to a stop outside the cabin. I ran harder through the forest, branches scraping my skin and clothing, until I reached the bike. Panting furiously, I started it up and raced away to the safety of the cabin by the river.

Back at the getaway cabin, I processed what I knew.

From Dan's email, I learned several important things. One, I now knew the name of the person in the grainy screenshot — the older man leering at Jill. To my surprise, he was the philanthropist, and billionaire owner of Mahigan — a Mr. Charles Pendleton. The FBI will try, I am certain, to find a connection between him and the sex trafficking ring. This will be very difficult, I must admit, given the only physical evidence is a photo of Pendleton sitting by the pool, hardly a smoking gun. Without more — physical evidence or a money trail — he is untouchable. I doubt that Janet will flip on him, and he is too smart, and well-resourced, to leave a trail. It is a dead end, and the thought made my blood boil.

The second bit of important news is that the FBI is following the money — payments secreted through multiple transactions involving offshore accounts — to the firm, which landed in a generic escrow account. The FBI suspected that it was payment to Janet for sandbagging the case against the resort upper management, and covering up their involvement in criminal activities. More digging is necessary to connect Janet to the money which, as Dan implied in the email, will be a very difficult, time consuming task.

For now, Grubbs is the only direct link to criminal activity at the resort. It is possible that he, Janet, or one or more of the thugs might flip on Pendleton, but I wasn't counting on it. The risk is just too great, and self-preservation is everyone's goal.

The bottom line, I now know with certainty, is that this is far from over. Pendleton is untouchable, and can hire an infinite number of thugs to do his dirty work. I, however, am what they call a "loose end," and we all know, from TV and the movies, that it never ends well for loose ends.

My stomach clenched. Will I ever get out of this mess? And what about Jill? Will she remain vulnerable?

I must do something.

I suppose my mind, like an overloaded breaker switch, had popped, because it suddenly went blank — taking my body with it, and sending me moments later into a long, dreamless sleep.

CHAPTER 27

I woke up the next morning with a plan. It was a half-baked one, borne of desperation, but still, it was a plan. I reasoned it must have been brewing in the far reaches of my mind while I slept, crashing through some invisible barrier to take center stage when I awoke.

I was tired of running.

With a cup of strong black coffee in hand, I searched Laura's guestroom for spare clothes. We are about the same size, which is incredibly fortunate given the circumstances. I found a shirt that fit and then rummaged through her dresser drawers, finding a faded pair of denim pants, and a maroon cashmere, crewneck sweater. I hit the jackpot, sorting through her closet again, with her assortment of expensive jackets, when I came across a dark brown Italian leather jacket — soft, warm, and perfect for this day, one that had broken cool and clear.

Since I was in debt to her and Tony for what it would take several lifetimes to repay, I figured a few items of clothing would not make a difference.

I wolfed down a plate of fried eggs, Canadian bacon, and an English muffin smothered in butter and strawberry jam. The calories were needed today — and it tasted incredible.

It was a few minutes before nine, with time ticking, so I grabbed a pen and pad of paper and wrote down the key elements of my plan. It always helped to write things out to organize my thoughts. Today, planning might mean the difference between life and death. Still, there are too many unknown variables to my liking, and so much can go wrong. It is my best chance, though, to find justice, and for me to get out from under the fear of being pursued for the rest of my life.

I must take the fight to them.

I sat down at Laura's desk and fired up her computer. The IP address on this computer was not linked to me, and although nothing was impossible, it was within a reasonable range of probability that no one could trace it to me, and find my location.

A google search of Charles Pendleton brought up too many pages to count. There were countless stories about his philanthropy, large gifts to tons of worthy charities, as well as stories on some of his hobbies, and interests in horses, literature, and fine wine. There was even a story about the possibility he might run for a seat on the United States Senate.

It made me sick to my stomach to see this monster portrayed as the perfect gentleman. We certainly didn't need a politician of his ilk. I resisted reading more than a few headlines, as I only needed one piece of information, and found it near the bottom of the page — his address.

I am going to pay Mr. Charles Pendleton a visit.

It was madness with way too many uncertainties. *Will he even be home?* If not, my plan was pointless.

And can I even get into his compound? I knew that security would be tight and could see from the photos taken by the paparazzi a large iron gate, manned round the clock, protected the front entrance, while a back gate, operated by remote control, guarded entry and exit from the rear. Surrounding the property was a tall iron fence, topped with sharp, ornamental spikes, which would deter even the most intrepid intruder.

I would most likely need to use charm and wit to gain entry, but would play it by ear.

It was imperative that I talked with Dan. But how? I had used my last burner phone.

I rummaged through the desk drawers, and was rewarded with the sight of an older model iPhone. Laura must have left it there for emergencies. It was perfect. Laura had once again saved the day. I plugged it in, and it came to life.

Now for the passcode, I thought. *What could it be?* Laura liked to keep things simple. I typed the digits of her birthday — day and month. Nothing. I typed the year she was born. Nothing. It was time to change tack. *Could it be that simple*, I asked myself, and typed in the last four digits of her phone number. With a sigh of relief, I saw the home screen come to life with an array of icons, telling me I was in.

Taking a deep breath, I hesitated, then called my one trusted ally, Dan.

"Hi Dan. This is Renee," I said, silently forming the words to explain the crazy idea I had in mind.

"Hi Renee. What is happening? Did you get my email?"

"I did, and thank you."

"I hope it's quiet at your hideaway. I'm glad you're staying safe and flying under the radar."

"About that…" I said, knowing that my next words would commit me to a course of action that could easily end in disaster.

"Oh no," he responded. "I know you well enough by now to suspect that you are doing some 'out of the box' thinking. I only hope that it doesn't put you in danger."

My pulse quickened, from the anxiety associated with what I was planning, but also from Dan becoming more intimate with me — knowing and anticipating my thoughts.

"I'm planning on paying a visit to Mr. Pendleton."

The phone went silent for a beat, and then Dan said the unexpected. "Go on. What is your plan?"

I told him — laying out a "Swiss cheese" plan that was so full of holes it sounded implausible even to me.

"OK," was all he said, and then, "I'll round up the cavalry. Give me until 11 a.m. before you attempt to enter the compound, so I can work with the FBI to have their agents in place."

"Thank you," I said, letting out an involuntary sigh. "I must ask, though, why are you so supportive of this half-baked plan?"

"Because it is more "baked" than you might think. The FBI has wanted to get into Pendleton's compound for a while now, given other criminal activities they suspect might be tied to him. The bar is high though, since Pendleton has judges and politicians on his payroll, preventing them from successfully arguing probable cause, and getting a warrant to search the premises. If you enter the compound, wired of course, and there are signs of foul play, they will have reason to raid Pendleton's home. It scares me to my toes though, that you will be putting yourself in danger. Please be careful."

"I will," I replied without conviction, knowing that it would be dangerous even under the best of circumstances.

"Give me an hour to pull the troops together. That is my only request."

"I'll do that. And Dan…"

"What?" he replied.

"Never mind," I said, thinking better of what I was about to say. "Just… Thank you."

An hour later, having mentally prepared for whatever lay ahead, I locked up the cabin and headed out the door.

Adrenaline coursed through my veins as I dashed across the yard and hopped on the Harley. With the helmet firmly attached to my head — I owed that thing my life and knew its importance beyond a doubt — I throttled the engine and took off down the trail.

Instead of heading toward the main road, I worked my way back toward Laura's cabin and parked the bike several hundred yards away in the woods. I crept through the woods and approached the shed where the Harley had been parked earlier. I found the bug just where I had left it, hidden in a jar of nails on the top shelf. The dusty old jar was undisturbed, a stroke of luck, meaning that the bad guys had not come back here to investigate after the close call yesterday.

Now is the time to use this device to my advantage, as the pied piper of bad guys, I thought, smiling, as I headed back to the bike.

I tossed the transponder into the carry compartment, then gunned the engine and tore off down the old logging road toward my destiny. "Come and get me," I yelled, my voice lost over the roar of the engine.

As I rode toward the Pendleton's mansion, I was soon filled with self-doubt. My plan, on its face, was crazy. I would meet with this Mr. Pendleton, use his arrogance and overconfidence to tease out his complicity in the sex trafficking business, and secretly record our conversation with a tiny recording device that fit into a small hole that I had cut into the lining of Laura's leather jacket. Dan had given it to me at the courthouse, saying that it might come in handy when talking privately with Janet. She had been too smart and cautious to say anything truly damaging, and then the case had come to an abrupt halt, ending any opportunity to speak with her further — and record her surreptitiously.

Dan had agreed to have the cavalry on standby — and I assumed they would be positioned close to the front gate of Pendleton's mansion.

With the tracking device back in motion, I hoped that the bad guys would notice and, seeing that I was heading for the compound, come running. I wanted them all to be together when the FBI came to the rescue. My plan was based on assumptions though — that the bad guys were still monitoring the tracking device, that they were still in the area, and that they would come to the compound, or already be there. Also, if they weren't there yet, and were coming, it was essential that I find my way into the compound before they arrived.

Dan was just being nice in saying that my plan is reasonable, I mused. It *was* a half-baked plan, and you know what they say about assumptions — but it was the best I could do under the circumstances.

As I approached the compound, I could see there was only one road leading to it. I saw no sign of the cavalry, Dan, and the FBI agents along the way, which I took as either a good or bad sign. They either had been held up or weren't coming for some reason, or were well hidden and out of sight of the bad guys, ready to make their move when the time was right.

Riding down the single lane road, I passed the main gate, feigning disinterest but taking everything in. The place, I could see, was a virtual fortress. There was no way I was climbing over that wall — and the guard at the gate looked hard as stone. My gut told me that no amount of sweet talking would get me in.

I drove on until I reached a point where the road ended in a cul-de-sac. Off to the right, and adjacent to Pendleton's estate was an empty lot with a house in the beginning stages of construction. Next to the outline of the foundation, and about fifteen to twenty feet from the wall, sat a huge mound of dirt, clearly there from when they dug the foundation.

For a moment, I was brought back to my BMX days, pounding over a rough dirt track, flying high over man-made ridges, and landing roughly to the earth, tires spinning and dirt flying. It was a great memory.

It also carried an insane idea with it. *What if I used that mound of dirt to launch my bike over the wall and into the compound,* the daredevil part of my brain considered. *It will be fun,* the even crazier part of my brain teased. *Bad idea. Stupid Idea,* the mature, safety-conscious part of my brain countered.

In the end, 'crazy' won out. I drove off the road, and onto the empty construction site, mentally calculating distances, probabilities of success, and pushing away fear and indecision. I was not on a motocross motorbike, but the Harley certainly had the power and stability to mount the dirt pile and clear the top of the wall. It would be close, but there was a better-than-average chance that it would work.

The landing was another issue entirely though since I couldn't see over the wall. On this side of the property, the wall was composed of ten feet of rock, topped with a short iron fence with spikes on top. It was most likely built that way for privacy, given the housing that was being constructed so close to the estate.

A thought occurred to me, so I grabbed a long metal nail from the construction site and hurled it at the top of the fence. It found its mark, striking the metal, and setting off the flame of a spark. It confirmed my suspicion. The metal part of the fence was electrified. *Oh great,* I thought, *let's just up the degree of difficulty, why don't we? Maybe we could add a ring of fire while we're at it.*

Settling my mind, I rode back from the fence, finding a clear path and estimating the distance needed to build enough speed to clear it. A large pile of stone blocking the way made the decision easier. It was as far back as I could go.

Before I could change my mind, the bike came alive under me, a throaty roar coming from the engine as I pulled the throttle and eased it to full. Just as in my younger, daredevil days, when I jumped everything imaginable, that same feeling of giddiness combined with raw fear enveloped me. My mind achieved a laser focus, and I felt fully alive. My thighs tightly gripped the bike as, climbing the mound, I felt the change in pitch. The tires fought to find traction on the loose dirt, while climbing ever higher and maintaining critical momentum.

Then came the moment I both loved and feared. The bike exited the mound of dirt, its last connection to this planet, and flew, tires spinning, seeking firm ground.

It's going to be close, I thought, with confidence borne of experience.

The Harley was no BMX, and it was like riding the back of a Clydesdale, instead of a quarter horse, in a jumping contest. Still, the Harley performed admirably, and cleared the top of the fence, the back tire just grazing the top of a spike.

So far, so good.

The next stage of the ride was a different story entirely. The bike, while maintaining its forward momentum, dropped like a rock. The Harley hit the ground hard enough to rattle my bones and compress my spine, a feeling I can now share with those who ride bulls for a living.

Just like a bull rider, I could also sense when all control was lost, and I was at the mercy of fate. The tires bounced from the impact, sending me hurtling through the air, and landing in the grass, rolling as I was taught, to dissipate the force of impact. An evergreen bush finally stopped my forward motion. The bike, for its part, cartwheeled forward, landing some distance away, at rest on its side.

As the old saying goes: 'any landing is a good landing.'

CHAPTER 28

OK, I thought. So much for stealth.

Taking stock, I laid still for a moment. A searing pain shot through my shoulder, and my right hip stung like crazy, resulting in what I knew would be a nasty bruise. The leather jacket was a bit roughed up, but that, and my trusty helmet, had saved me from any serious cuts, scrapes, or worse.

Standing on shaky legs, I moved unsteadily toward the house, brushing grass and dirt from my jacket and jeans, and pulling off my helmet, allowing a better view of my surroundings.

Have I lost my mind? I was walking into the lion's den, battered and bruised, with no assurance of backup. Who knew if Dan was able to round up the FBI agents? I hadn't seen any sign of them.

I pushed through a dense hedge of evergreens until I had the colossal home clear in my sights.

Unfortunately, a group of very tough looking armed men had *me* in their *sights*.

The leader, a tall man with a hard edge, dressed head to toe in black, and carrying an assault rifle, looked at me as if I were a stray dog, and simply said, "Follow me."

Heading toward the front door, with no-one laying a hand on me, I felt more like a formal house guest than someone who had just trespassed on the property of one of the wealthiest people on the East Coast.

As we reached the front door, my confidence had returned. Despite a slight limp, I regained my composure and looked not much worse for wear. Tempering my confidence, one of the armed guards frisked and wanded me while I held my breath. I slowly released it when no alarms had been raised, silently thanking Dan for a listening device that was undetectable to their security measures.

Mr. Charles Pendleton himself opened the door and ushered me inside. He was smoking a pipe, while adorned in a red silk robe. I hoped he had something on under it.

"Why, hello Dr. Strickland," he said smoothly. "It is so nice of you to visit. Won't you please come in? I'm sorry that you had to enter in such an inhospitable manner. You could have just come through the front gate, you know."

Facing this extremely powerful and completely corrupt man, I said, nonchalantly, "I fancied a little adventure today. Perhaps I'll take you up on that offer the next time I visit."

Pendleton smiled at the comment, respect showing in his eyes as he sized me up. "Let us adjourn to the sitting room. Bertram will bring us some tea and refreshments — unless, of course you would prefer something stronger."

"No thank you," I replied. "That will be …" My voice caught, as I entered the room to see none other than *Janet* — reclining on the couch as if she didn't have a care in the world.

"Well, well. If it isn't Elvira Knievel, the motorcycle stunt queen," she said, her voice dripping with sarcasm. "We watched it all on the security camera. It was quite the show. You look as though you had a rough landing. Did you break anything?"

"Now, Janet," Pendleton interjected, "let's show better manners to our guest. I think she looks quite lovely, in a rugged sort of way."

The way he said this, with a hint of malice and lust in his voice, both disgusted and scared the hell out of me. Where were Dan and the FBI?

"Let's all have a spot of tea, and let our emotions settle. The trial may not have ended the way you had hoped, Janet, but the FBI can't reach us. Our connection to the operation is too thin, and well hidden, to ever stick."

"What operation?" I asked, taking a long sip of the tea. "How were you using the resort for trafficking?" I had momentum, and decided to get all the information from him I could.

Pendleton answered, as if speaking to a child. "My dear Dr. Strickland, I know you wouldn't be here without some sort of listening device on your person. It could be anywhere on you, but I felt it would be in bad taste to strip-search a guest. So, I took you into this room, one where, as you may have noticed, is smaller than most, and almost square in shape. It is a structure within a structure — the larger home — a Faraday cage, if you will. As a person of learning, you should know the purpose of a Faraday cage, a place where no electronic signals can be sent or received."

My heart sank. How could I have ever been so naïve as to think that I would have the upper hand with my foolish ploy.

"Also," added Pendleton, "you will notice the room moving now, as it sinks two floors below the main level of the house. The FBI agents, whom I am certain you have invited to the house, will not be able to find you. Your bike, and any evidence of your having entered the compound, has been all but erased."

The feeling of despair that had so strongly bounded me now turned to raw fear. I rose to fight, perhaps finding some way to escape, but my legs wouldn't move. I could speak, but my body refused to obey any commands sent by my brain.

"What is happening to me?" I said with a raised voice, fueled by fear and anger. "We all drank from the same pot of tea. Why am I the only one who has been drugged?"

"Because, my dear, your *mug* had been laced with a chemical that causes temporary paralysis. It will wear off in no time. That will not only be fortunate for you, but also for a client who prefers his merchandise to be of an older vintage, and lively."

Merchandise? I thought, as my blood boiled. This was how people who were trafficked were viewed — not as people with hearts, souls, and minds, but as chattel, merchandise, property. It was disgusting, and purely evil.

Janet enjoyed my grim predicament, as evidenced by the smirk plastered on her face and her casual, relaxed posture. "Do you see what happens when we don't play by the rules of those with power, my dear? While I might not be a proponent of human trafficking, I do understand the financial benefits."

"You're a *partner* in all this?" I asked. This was surreal. "I thought Pendleton had just paid you to keep quiet and to sandbag the case against the resort."

"You are so perceptive," replied Janet, her voice again laced with sarcasm. "I guess that I'm the type that gives lawyers a bad name. But so be it. Charles and I will soon jet off to a place where we can live in comfort until things settle down. You, my dear, won't have it quite so good, as your ultimate destination will be at the bottom of a deep well once your expiration date comes due."

"Oh, my goodness," interjected Pendleton. "It has been a nice chat, but it looks like our visit is over."

I looked up to see my old nemesis Shrek enter the room. "So, we meet again, Dr. Strickland. I am here to take you on the first leg of your journey — somewhere warm, dry, and sandy, and quite a distance from here."

With blinding fear, I struggled with all my might, but no matter how hard I tried, just couldn't *will* my body to move.

The next thing I knew, Shrek had picked me up and slung me over his shoulder, unceremoniously removing me from the room, down a dimly lit hallway, and into the bowels of the mansion.

CHAPTER 29

Traveling through the maze of hallways in Pendleton's underground lair, I was soon completely disoriented. I could feel some sensation — a tingling feeling — returning to my legs, but they were still too sluggish to move. We rounded a final corner and entered a large bay, an area that serviced the many trucks that served the copious needs of the billionaire and his friends. It was also, as I soon found, an area for moving trafficked people in and out of the compound.

One of the cargo bay doors was open, with the back end of the semi inviting more 'goods' to be loaded. In this case, it was people. Ten to twelve young women, all appearing dazed and sluggish, were herded into the back of the truck by armed men, while I was carried in and tossed onto a soiled mattress.

"Enjoy the trip," said Shrek with a sneer. The door was closed and latched, leaving us all in utter darkness. I heard the truck start with a shudder, and soon we were rolling.

This is the end, I thought. A single tear rolled down my cheek as I considered the future, not only for me, but also for the young, terrified women sharing the truck compartment with me. I could literally smell the fear and despair. Human trafficking was certainly the evilest, and most horrible, of criminal endeavors.

I heard the gate rattle open, signaling our departure from the compound and into the unknown.

As I lay back on the dirty mattress, multiple escape scenarios ran through my head, all of them ending in failure. Distracted by these thoughts, the truck suddenly lurched to a stop, rolling me off the mattress, and sending several of the girls sprawling. What I heard next brought with it feelings of both hope and concern. It was the spatter of gunfire.

The truck lurched forward, only to finally stop again — this time for good.

Less than a minute later, the rear door swung open and daylight filled the cabin. I squinted, my eyes adjusting to the bright light, as the finest sight I could possibly imagine met my eyes. It was Dan, having hopped into the truck, bearing a grin that spread from ear to ear. He lifted me up on wobbly legs, now beginning to recover from the paralytic drug, and gave me a crushing hug. I cried unashamedly into his shoulder.

Once we were out of the truck and on firm ground, we walked over and sat on the back bumper of a waiting ambulance. Dan looked at me again with that famous grin. "Stirring up trouble again, are we? What are we going to do with you?"

"I had it all under control," I said sarcastically, not able to control what I thought might become a permanent smile.

"Seems that way. I think it's time to give *trouble* a break and stop chasing it, though."

"Speaking of trouble," I said hurriedly, the memory of Janet and Pendleton flooding back, "when I entered the mansion, I was led to a disguised Faraday cage, one that not only blocked electronic transmissions but also acted as some sort of improvised elevator, dropping several floors to the service entrance level. That floor is a maze of passageways, and I'm not sure if I could ever find my way back to the room."

"Like any smart rat," said Dan, "they probably have an escape route or two."

His words triggered a memory, and it took a few seconds — but then it hit me. The mound of dirt at the construction site — it was way larger than it should have been from preparing the foundation. What if…

"An exit tunnel," I said excitedly. "I think I know where one might be."

I told Dan my idea, and he quickly relayed it to the senior FBI special agent on site. A moment later, a slew of vehicles sped off in the direction of the construction site.

"I hope you're right," said Dan earnestly. "We seriously need to catch them."

An hour later, after a de-briefing with several special agents, Dan caught up with me and told me he had some news to share. I could tell by his demeanor that it was good news.

"You will be very glad to hear this," he said, bursting with eagerness to share what he knew.

"Your tip was met with great success. That billionaire, Pendleton, and my former crooked colleague, Janet, were caught coming out of a tunnel in the foundation of the construction site that we told the agents about. They had suitcases and backpacks, ready to make a getaway to some warm climate, no doubt — likely a secluded island that Pendleton owned, under the jurisdiction of another country."

"I'm sure they didn't plan to walk there," I said with a hint of sarcasm. "So how did they plan to get away?"

"We found a Bell Helicopter several lots down, hidden by a ridge running along the boundary to another property owned by Pendleton. It was fueled and ready for takeoff.

They hadn't made it fifty feet before they were apprehended. Pendleton tried to make a run for it but tripped on the cuff of his silk robe, landing in the dirt. Janet threatened a lawsuit, and the loss of the badges of the agents apprehending her, which of course was just a lot of hot air.

"With your testimony, along with that of the girls, the government should have enough to put Pendleton away for a long time, despite his wealth and power. He is also likely to rat out his partners, leading to the complete downfall of his criminal enterprise, not the least of which is the human trafficking ring. You, my dear, have saved not only the current victims, but also countless other future victims."

Sitting now on the curb of the loading dock, I looked closely at Dan and saw a fair and honest man, so much the opposite of Pendleton and his hired guns. The thought, though comforting, recalled one that was less pleasant. What had happened to Shr—

As my thought was abruptly cut off, several things happened at once — Dan shoved me flat, while inches above us, a barrage of bullets whipped past. The gunfight, furious and brief, ended with the sound of shell casings *pinging* off concrete, as Dan and I crouched beneath the loading dock bay, counting our blessings, happy to be alive.

When certain the danger had passed, I looked back to see Shrek lying on the floor, his crumpled body riddled with bullets. In the other direction, an agent was down, holding the shoulder a bullet had grazed.

"Did they find the Harley?" I asked, the first words spoken since this latest attack on my life, seeming out of context in the moment.

"Um, yeah," replied Dan.

"Want to go for a ride? I need to get away from this place."

Dan just nodded.

CHAPTER 30

"Dan," I said, as we sat together on the couch in front of a roaring fire enjoying a cup of fresh roasted coffee. "I could get used to this."

"So could I," said Dan, as he pulled me closer. "This cabin is amazing. Do you think that Laura and Tony would let you stay here for a while longer?"

"It couldn't hurt to ask," I replied.

Catching them when they weren't in transit, or attending some meeting or social event, was next to impossible, but I dialed Laura's number anyway.

It must have been my lucky day. Laura answered, telling me they had just arrived in Harbor Springs, Michigan, and were settling into their house in an exclusive enclave nearby.

After several minutes of small talk, I worked up the nerve to tell her about what had happened to her cabin and garage of fine automobiles. I also told her I had been staying at their getaway cabin.

"My gosh," said Laura, "I'm so glad that you're OK. Are you sure you weren't hurt?"

She hadn't skipped a beat when I told her about the damage and loss of their amazing vehicles. Her sole concern was for my welfare.

Choking back tears at her selflessness and concern for my welfare, I said, "I'm OK Laura. I'm just so sorry for what happened. I'm not sure I'll ever be able to make it up to you and Tony."

"Don't give it a second thought. Things can be replaced, but good friends can't. Besides, we have everything insured to the hilt, so we can make the necessary repairs and replacements."

I breathed a huge sigh of relief, knowing that I could never compensate them for the losses given my modest salary.

"I can at least be here to supervise the repairs, and ensure that everything is repaired and replaced the right way," I said, offering what I could to help.

"That would be wonderful," said Laura, taking me up on the offer. "We don't anticipate coming back there for another ten to twelve months, so you are welcome to stay at either cabin. And I'll put you in touch with someone on our staff who will be working with our insurance company and coordinating things remotely."

My heart lifted as I considered the implications of living in such a remote, beautiful place for the next year or so. "I can't thank you enough Laura," I said with an outpouring of emotion for my good friend. "I mean it!"

"Any time, my friend," replied Laura, ending the call.

That couldn't have gone better if I'd scripted it myself, I thought, as the stress melted away.

Noticing the change in my demeanor, Dan said, "I guess that went well."

"Very," was my only reply, my ear-to-ear grin putting an exclamation point on my feelings.

"Since we are tying up loose ends—" said Dan expectantly. "Maybe we should pay a visit to the Covington family. I don't know about you, but I would like to see them again. I also wanted to ask them if they want to re-file the negligence claim on behalf of Jill, given all that has happened recently."

"It couldn't hurt to ask," I replied, disappointed that the earlier case had resulted in a mistrial. "I'll call them now."

Aside from my brief interaction with Elaine, Jill, and Logan at the earlier trial, I hadn't spent any real time with the family. I found my hands trembled slightly as I picked up the phone to call them.

My call was answered by Elaine, who sounded more confident than when we had spoken briefly during Logan's trial.

"Hello," she said, "This is Elaine. And who is this?"

"This is Dr. Strickland, um Renee. Do you have a moment?"

"A moment," Elaine said with a snort. "I have all the time in the world for you, Dr. Strickland. In fact, I was going to call you, but thought you might need some time alone after all that's happened."

"I'm OK," I said, and meant it. "Do you think we could all get together sometime soon?"

"If you mean me and my family, absolutely!" replied Elaine, genuinely delighted by the prospect.

"Would it be OK with you all if Dan came as well?"

"Of course," said Elaine. "I know it's last minute, but we planned to go out for lunch today. There is a great pizza place in town that has a buffet. You both are welcome to join us. Would noon work for you all?"

"That sounds perfect. We'll meet you there."

"See you then," replied Elaine, and soon we headed out, arriving at the restaurant a few minutes late after some misdirection from our navigation app.

The restaurant was typical for a local Italian place of good quality, with dim lighting, checkered tablecloths, and the rich scent of wood-fired pizza, simmering red sauce, and fresh baked bread greeting our senses.

A large booth in the back corner, occupied by the Covington family caught our attention, as Jerry Covington got up and came over to greet us.

After introductions, Dan and I slipped into the booth with the family and sat down, momentarily in awkward silence. Dan broke the silence, saying, "So, what's good here? Logan, you look like a pizza expert. What do you recommend?"

Logan, his face lighting up from the confidence this adult had placed in him said, without hesitation, "I would go with the pepperoni. It's my favorite."

"Pepperoni it is, then," said Dan, eliciting a big smile from Logan.

"Thanks for seeing us," I said, helping to create a Segway to some of the things we wanted to share.

"Of course," said Jerry. "It is our pleasure."

"You have some very brave kids," I said, stating the obvious. "It takes a lot of courage to stand up for yourselves, in the face of so much adversity."

It was difficult for me to form the right words, as anything I could say felt inadequate, given the enormity of all that had happened.

Jerry and Elaine simply sat silent, anticipating something significant might be coming.

The opening was there, and Dan took it.

"I have some thoughts that I want to run by you — as a family, since it will involve all of you. Please know that there is absolutely no pressure, though."

"OK," said Jerry. "We're listening."

The table fell silent as all eyes were on Dan in anticipation of his words.

"As you know, Jill's case was declared a mistrial. After the dust settled, and thanks to the heroic and selfless efforts of Renee, the bad guys have been apprehended."

Elaine reached across the table and grabbed my hands, her eyes welling up with tears of gratitude.

Dan paused, giving the moment the time it needed, and then continued.

"I realize this is a lot to put on your plate, given all you've been through, but our firm would like the opportunity to try Jill's case again."

A moment passed, and then Jerry asked, "But it was declared a mistrial. I didn't think we would get another chance."

"You have," said Dan in a matter-of-fact tone, "because we now have a new defendant, Mr. Charles Pendleton, the owner of the resort, who we now know was directly involved in the trafficking activities."

Jill flinched at the words, clearly taking her back to the terror and despair she had felt the night of her abduction. Her face had lost all emotion.

To everyone's surprise, the next words came from Logan. "My sister is tough, smart, and brave. And she never backs down. You should have seen her when I ate the last cookie last night."

"It was the cookies and cream type. My favorite, you little brat," said Jill with a playful smile.

Something about that simple brother-sister bantering choked me up as we all laughed at her response.

In the next instant, Jill's smile had vanished, to be replaced with a steely resolve.

"I'm in," she said, "but you all should know that my decision is not based on greed. I want money from the case to go toward ending the disgusting practice of human trafficking. I also want to help advance the science on injury prevention and treatment. There is a lot of work that needs to be done on both fronts and I want to support that."

This statement brought smiles from everyone at the table, as well as nods of appreciation and pride from her parents. The Covingtons had, without a doubt, some very special kids.

"Great," said Dan. "Now for the important stuff, taking care of this delicious-looking pepperoni pizza."

There was agreement all around as everyone tucked into their slice of the mouthwatering pizza.

Over the ensuing months, I enjoyed the comfort and solitude of the cabin while working remotely on sabbatical, a deal the university had offered when they heard about what I had endured, and the risks that I had taken in helping to bring down the notorious human trafficking ring.

Mr. Pendleton, and his accomplices — including that evil snake, Janet — had been tried and convicted on multiple counts for their trafficking activities. Add to that, kidnapping, attempted murder, and conspiracy to commit murder. They would all be serving life sentences.

Jill's civil case was filed again, with Pendleton now a named defendant. I wasn't involved since my testimony would now be considered tainted, given the circumstances surrounding my prior involvement. It didn't matter though, as the case settled before trial for a figure well into the millions.

A few months after the settlement was finalized, Dan and I met for dinner with the Covingtons — this time at the Mahigan Resort.

We arrived at the newly renovated dining room in Mahigan's best restaurant. This time, Elaine, Jerry, and the kids were waiting for us at the entrance. Logan was walking now with minimal assistance, his only aid a stylish cane with a silver handle. We soon reached our table, one reserved for us next to a large bay window. Once seated, several waiters appeared from nowhere and, treating us like royalty, met our every need.

"So," said Dan, with a huge grin, "it looks like the Covington family is moving up in the world."

Elaine, looking like a new person with the weight of the world removed from her shoulders, replied, "Yes, yes we have."

"I'm so happy for you," I said with all sincerity. "You all, more than anyone, deserve this."

"Whether we deserve it or not," said Jerry, "I have to admit that it doesn't suck."

"We haven't told you," said Elaine, but we are now part owners in the resort. "We even had that horrible top floor completely renovated and turned into a large apartment. We can come here whenever we want and enjoy living in the lap of luxury."

"But these are just a few of the benefits. There is more that we wanted to share. But first, let's have a toast."

We all raised our glasses, some filled with fine wine, and others with water or soda, as Jerry made a toast. "To our good friends, Dan, and Renee, who made this possible. We thank you from the bottom of our hearts."

Glasses clinked and sips were taken, but before the glasses were lowered, I chimed, "And to the bravest people on the planet, Jill, and Logan. You are both amazing."

Glasses were raised and clinked again as everyone beamed with joy and amusement.

"The best part of all is still to come," said Elaine, as we settled into our appetizers, a delicious sampling of one of everything on the menu. "Jill, why don't you tell us."

Jill, with maturity beyond her age, said, "Thank you, Mother. I'll start with what we've done here at the resort. We've placed an emphasis on making this a safe, family friendly resort, in every way. To that end, we would like to offer you, Dr. Strickland, the job of conducting periodic facility safety audits. Would you be willing?"

"Of course," I replied. "I would love to do that."

"Great," said Jill. "Next, in the interest of having an inclusive resort, we are placing an emphasis on making it fully accessible for people with disabilities. This was Logan's idea, and one that we wholeheartedly support."

"That is fantastic," said Dan.

"In addition to our ownership interest in the resort and the improvements we are making," Jill continued, "we have created our own foundation — The Covington Family

Foundation — to address the problem of human trafficking and support those who have been victimized. The foundation will also support research into finding a cure for spinal injuries."

"Wow," was all I could say, as words escaped me. It was wonderful to see good overcome evil, in the face of such overwhelming odds.

The remainder of the evening went by too fast, with great food and conversation. An unbreakable bond had formed between us. All too soon, we said our goodbyes and made our way toward the car. Halfway through the lobby, I stopped, and turned to look back, watching the Covington family exit the restaurant, laughing and joking among themselves.

Score one for the legal profession, I thought with satisfaction. This time, justice has been served, and the world is a better place for it.